CEREMONY OF INNOCENCE

Ceremony of Innocence

Tears, Power and Protest

Kay Carmichael

Consultant Editor
Jo Campling

St. Martin's Press New York

First published in the United States of America in 1991

Printed in Hong Kong

ISBN 0–312–05699–0

Library of Congress Cataloging-in-Publication Data
Carmichael, Kay.
Ceremony of innocence : tears, power, and protest / Kay Carmichael
consultant editor, Jo Campling.
    p. cm.
Includes bibliographical references (p.) and index.
ISBN 0–312–05699–0
    1. Crying. 2. Crying—Case studies. 3. Nonverbal communication
(Psychology) 4. Emotional conditioning. I. Title.
BF575.C88C37 1991
153.6'9—dc20   90–27705
                                                              CIP

To my tutors in pain

Contents

Acknowledgements

No book is ever written by one person alone. The most important contributors to this one have been the women and men who have given me permission to describe the pain which for many of them had lain hidden for years at the heart of their lives. Sometimes the same story was told by a number of people, only the words used varied. I have asked permission to quote each person whose words I have used.

My thanks go also to the specialists of various disciplines whom I approached for advice and guidance. After initial surprise that anyone should be seriously interested in a subject like tears, they could not have been more helpful. Jo Campling, Frances Condick and Belinda Dutton have proved a model combination of professionalism and caring.

While writing the book I was surrounded by loving support from a number of people, each of whom made a different contribution to its development: Sheena Carmichael who revived my spirit whenever it flagged; David Donnison who tried to teach me how to write in paragraphs, an art which still eludes me; David Brandon, my favourite Buddhist monk and story-teller; Susan Singerman who has taught me so much about survivors; Duncan Forrester of New College; David and Christine Martin, Larry Butler and Mary Troup. Each of them has enriched the book. I owe an intellectual debt to Professor Silvan Tomkins from whose thinking I borrowed heavily, and a debt for which there are no easy words to Cam Macdonald, beloved physician, friend and teacher who was so generous with his time and knowledge.

Those of you who read as far as the epilogue will appreciate the remarkable contribution to my understanding of the power of tears, and to my life made by the Reverend Usami of the Kemboko Temple. I would also like to thank the Sasakawa Foundation for their help in making my journey to Japan possible.

Grateful acknowledgement is made for permission to quote from the following works: 'The Second Coming' by W. B. Yeats from *Selected Poetry* (ed. A. N. Jeffares) (London: Macmillan, 1962); 'On the day my mind stopped breathing', and 'Cuckoo' from *Journeys of Nothing in the Land of Everything* by Edward Matchett (London: Turnstone Books, 1975); 'The Box' from *The Barbarian File* by

Christopher Wiseman (Windsor, Ontario: 1974); 'Little Gidding' from *Four Quartets* by T. S. Eliot in *The Complete Poems and Plays of T. S. Eliot* (London: Faber and Faber, 1969); and Henry Holt and Co., Inc. for an extract from 'Rendezvous' from *Mink Coat* by Jill Hoffmann (New York: Holt, Rinehart and Winston, 1969).

Turning and turning in the widening gyre
The falcon cannot hear the falconer;
Things fall apart; the centre cannot hold;
Mere anarchy is loosed upon the world,
The blood-dimmed tide is loosed, and everywhere
The ceremony of innocence is drowned;

W. B. Yeats

Prologue

Some years ago I visited a transit camp for refugees from Vietnam in Hong Kong. To reach it we had driven through a raucous, lively area of that town which vibrates with vitality. Suddenly turning into a narrow dusty lane, we arrived in a different world. An old army barracks, cut off from the town by a wire fence topped with barbed wire, lay ahead. It was a massive four-storey, grey, rectangular building surrounded by a concrete pathway and divided along its length by fetid drains. 200 families lived here in primitive conditions, looked after by a tiny group of devoted but often helpless paid staff, and some voluntary workers. The Vietnamese waited patiently but often unrealistically for opportunities to enter countries which would give them the chance to work and make new lives for themselves and their children.

There were few adults about, most of them officials, and some apparently aimless children. One small girl was standing by herself outside the security guard's hut, weeping bitterly. She looked to be about three years of age. Her nose was running, her mouth was open, deep sobs racked her body and no one took the slightest notice of her. She was a scrap of humanity in deepest misery and as far as the adults in her environment were concerned, she might as well not have existed. Yet her whole self was in despair and no one moved towards her. I found her pain intolerable, ultimately moved towards her while asking our guide to explain why she was crying, at which she was picked up and hurried off. When I next saw her she was still weeping, though more quietly now and being dragged along reluctantly by a small boy of about six who had clearly been charged with the care of her.

That night I woke up weeping and was forced to confront yet again the pain I had carried with me for over half a century . . . the pain of the uncomforted child. I was crying for myself and not for her. I had known, looking at her, exactly what she was feeling. The differences in our ages, the different colour of our skins, or the shape of our eyes, our different interpretations of the sounds that make words, all these were irrelevant. We were two creatures linked by a special kind of pain. Not only us. Everyone for whom that experience has gone on too long knows exactly what I mean. For them, what in most people's lives is a temporary hurt has developed into a wound, a wound for which there is no healing other than in its acceptance.

In that child, and other children I saw in the hours I spent in the camp, that wound was just in the process of being formed. They needed what I too had needed, a person of one's own to ward off fear and to give comfort, a place with that person that they can take for granted, that they don't need always to be fighting for, that is theirs without question or resentment. For some of them it was already too late to heal their wounds. The pain had been so great that they had turned away from it, covered it over with thick layers of assumed indifference, latent anger, cynicism, toughness, survival skills. There were remnants of it in the tension around their eyes, the same tension you can spot in some of the children in any children's home in this country. Others were still in touch with their pain, still able to weep, still alive, and therefore still open to the possibility of being healed.

I realized too as I came out of my nightmare that for me the time had passed when I could expect to be healed. Not that I had denied my wound: indeed I had worked quite hard at keeping it alive. Only by maintaining contact with it was I able to engage as a social worker in helping other people to be healed. I had tried to avoid the traps of professionalism, of habit, of taking refuge in detachment. I had tried to let the world come through me rather than round me. I realized too that I would have to go on for the rest of my life carrying it and that all I could now try to do was bear it with some decency and dignity. I should not look to anyone to heal it for me because it is no-one else's responsibility to do that. Nor should I blame anyone else for not being able to heal it for me. Most of my friends have their own wounds to attend to.

I began to understand too, that I mustn't pretend that it doesn't exist or that now that I understand, everything will be all right. There will be times when it will continue to overwhelm me, when I feel I'm drowning in it and the pain is unbearable. But I know that I'll survive. I can think of my pain as an old friend and say 'Hello friend', you've come again – some day I might even be able to say 'Welcome', just as some day I hope I can welcome my death. Perhaps my dying will be a form of healing the wound. I will be reunited with the source of the pain and it will disappear. Until now I have built my life by appearing confident, cheerful, good-humoured, friendly, even loving, over an abyss of terror.

I am only one of many who have learned to live in this way. Our route has been different, but all of us began in the same way, innocently crying out to the world for help, for comfort, for relief from the terror of being alone and abandoned. In any High Street, where a child has been left in a pram and wakened to find herself alone surrounded by strange images you can see the face of terror. It is flushed and contorted into an expression of agony; the screaming if allowed to go on becomes choked and hysterical. Children can look and sound as if they are in the third layer of hell. If an adult stood in the street and screamed with that degree of terror everyone would be halted in their tracks and a doctor or ambulance would be called. But when a baby screams in distress, most people don't even notice. We develop selective blindness and deafness.

One or even two experiences like that are not going to damage a fundamentally healthy relationship between a child and its parents, but a steady diet of learning that you cannot command loving care and relief from distress, that the adult is not there for you, wears away all confidence in the world.

Each of us carries our own memories of tears: tears of panic, tears of terror, tears of anxiety, grief and betrayal. For each of us who have outgrown childhood, the triggers that move us to tears are different. Different things have power over us. My house could burn down and I would walk away without a tear, but if I stumble and fall in the street I have to fight back tears. A complex story lies behind my fear of helplessness and having no one to comfort me. I used to think there was a child within me, crying all the time, waiting to be seen and heard.

I was sent as a pupil to the convent of St Joseph of Cluny, in Ayrshire. All the nuns had to be called 'Mother', with the exception of the Reverend Mother, a charming but remote figure. I had no idea where my own mother had disappeared to when she left me there. One of the nuns, Mother Stanislaus, took a 'particular' interest in me. At four and a half, I was the smallest child. Whenever visitors were being shown around the school, she would send for me. Standing me in front of her she would say to the visitors, 'Watch this', hold her forefinger up in front of my nose and I would burst into tears like a performing monkey. I remember so clearly how I used to try not to do what she wanted, but always the tears and misery overflowed. I have often wondered what it was about me that fuelled her sadism.

For many children, childhood is a nightmare from which they

never recover. Children are constantly betrayed. Sometimes in the dramatic forms of being abandoned permanently but sometimes in simpler ways. Children are lied to, bullied, roughly handled as their clothes are impatiently put on and taken off, shouted at and shaken. And all this is done by people whom the child loves with every fibre of her body. If that is not betrayal, what is?

It is not surprising then that betrayal is a recurring theme for many people, which invokes tears but often tears mixed with anger and the desire for revenge. Being beaten by someone who loves you is an act of betrayal which makes the beaten child – from Hitler to the abused child next door – stalk the world seeking revenge. To be abandoned is to be betrayed. To have your secrets, told in confidence to a friend, told to another, is to be betrayed. Where a contract of sexual fidelity is made, infidelity is a betrayal. But so can be a look or a touch, a betrayal not of sexual fidelity but of a commitment deeper and stronger than sexual fidelity – a spiritual trust.

The deepest sense of betrayal does not inspire revenge but withdrawal. The desire for revenge implies a continuing link with the one who has betrayed you, and sometimes the pain is too great for that. This is the difference between those who commit murder and those who kill themselves. Those who commit murder are still seeking love and connection. The others have given up hope. Themes of death, suicide and murder stalk through every childhood and wait to flower in adult life.

The key to heal these wounds lies in the ability to comfort the child. No one is more generous than a young child, no one has a greater capacity to forgive and respond to comfort if it is offered quickly after the insult has been offered. My experience, and the experience of many others, of being comforted while crying is not a happy one. As adults we are very unsure about accepting comfort. It may be because it was not given to us when we needed it, or because it was given to us erratically and inconsistently. For myself I prefer to go off like a wounded animal and cry alone, and simply see myself through experiences of distress. I have learned from some people that it doesn't need to be like that, but find it hard to believe.

The ability to comfort each other is insufficiently understood as a human function. It may need to be taught. Lucky children learn it from their mother or father, but some parents have never been comforted themselves and don't know how to offer it to their own children. My memory of my own mother was that she could not comfort me, because whatever happened to me was never as bad as what was happening to her. But my grandmother comforted me and from her I learnt enough to be able to comfort my mother when she asked that of me, and in the course of time to comfort my own child too. But we can only give to others what we were given ourselves. We all know partners or parents who, if you complain of not feeling well, immediately find that they too have something wrong with them. Competitiveness for attention and comfort within the family leads to desperate conflict and misunderstanding.

It is perhaps not surprising that the child in the Hong Kong camp was left to cry uncomforted. Her parents, living in their crowded cages, had probably little to offer. But while we can understand her parents' problems, while we may even forgive them for their neglect, I'm not sure if we should forgive those of us who turn our faces aside and collude with the conditions which create that camp and all the other camps in the world through which children wander uncomforted.

1

Introduction

What our civilization needs to-day as a condition for increasing
human maturity and for inner renewal, is the cultivation of an
exquisite sensitivity and an incomparable tenderness ... Un-
nameable horrors have paraded before us and worse evils
threaten because we have been unable to wipe the blank stare of
indifference from our stony tearless faces. We are too numb even
to hate what is hateful. Lacking the capacity to feel, when feeling
is an imperative condition for living on a human plane, we also
lack the capacity for action.

Lewis Mumford, *The Conduct of Life*

We cry from infancy to death. We sing about tears, write poems
about them, but rarely talk or write about our own experiences and
what crying, weeping and the shedding of tears means to us. I
couldn't understand why, so I began to talk to people, first
individual women whom I knew, then groups of women in health
workshops and in self-help groups. I soon found out that while
tears may not have been written about it wasn't because they were
not interesting ... to women at any rate. They poured out their
thoughts and feelings about why they cried, where they cried,
when they cried. At the first workshop we held, the atmosphere
was electric.

It was as if we women had been given permission for the first
time in our lives to share something powerful and important. I can
still feel how my skin prickled with the energy generated in the
room. It was here I first sensed the healing quality that tears can
bring to someone suffering. One woman in the group, who had
taken no part in the discussion began to cry, quietly and gently. No
one said anything, but the women near her moved closer and put
their arms round her. It was a moving and touching experience
and many of the rest of us felt tears coming to our eyes. After the

meeting she wrote to tell me what an important and healing experience the group had given her. Crying alone, as she had always done, usually resulted in her feeling drained and lonely. This time she felt supported and encouraged.

At first I thought tears were only important to women. I was wrong. I discovered that, given the opportunity, many men were as eager as women to talk about their tears and how, when and where they cry. Often their only release was at the cinema, theatre or while watching television. What they feared most was that their tears would not be respected; they would be laughed at or they would be seen as weak. Only the strongest and most courageous could speak easily about their impulses to cry. Some men express-ed a sense of anger that women have so much more freedom to express feelings. They didn't realize that there are also women whose lives have been pervaded with a sense of shame whenever they have been forced into tears.

If our tears make us uncomfortable, we find it difficult to see other people cry, particularly in public places. We avert our eyes as if they were doing something indecent or obscene. Even if we know the person and know the reason for their behaviour – it might be a recent bereavement – we're still uncomfortable. Many of us will cross the street to avoid having to face their distress. It's as if we ourselves are threatened. With a stranger it's even worse: we may even become indignant that they should embarrass us in this way. Yet my childhood memories are full of images of drunk Glasgow men weaving their way home on a Saturday night from the pub, singing weepy, nostalgic songs who, if they found a shoulder to lean on, would cry noisily and pathetically.

Our attitude to our tears is built into us at a very early age, first by our parents and later by teachers, employers and any figures of authority whom we encounter. Our friends, exposed to the same guilts and taboos, share our feelings. To help me understand this process, I began to draw on my own experiences and memories – always a painful task, which, for all the years I've been doing it, doesn't get any easier. I tried to remember also the life stories of others who have for shorter or longer periods of time shared a path with me. I realized that we cry from infancy to death but under-stand practically nothing about the process. I went back and re-read the Bible, that most marvellous source of human experi-ence. I found the Old Testament brimming over with references to tears, weeping and crying. Texts of wisdom from faiths other than

Christianity were the same. I discovered myself reading novels and poetry with a fresh eye and finding constant references to this undiscussed subject. I began to listen to songs and found in the BBC Glasgow music library more than 200 songs listed with 'tears' or 'crying' in the title. The invisible subject was gradually becoming visible.

I began to sense that the part tears and crying play in childhood, and the way they teach us to deal with the world, is important for the establishment of healthy, caring and democratic relationships between people and therefore of a healthy, caring and democratic society. Tears are an important symbol of our humanity, a touchstone of our capacity to feel hurt for our own sakes but also to feel hurt for others.

Most are triggered by our suffering, and all suffering seems to arise from three primary sources which are part of the human condition. The most powerful of these is our mortality, the transient fleeting nature of all things, particularly our own lives. Virgil spoke of these tears: '. . . and mortality her tears. The woes of man touch the heart.' We have all to come to terms with our physical vulnerability as we walk erect through the world carrying everything that makes us function inside a fragile skull balanced on a tube down our spine, with the knowledge that our death is inevitable.

The second is our need for other people. No matter how much we pretend to be independent, we are from birth linked into relationships. These may be good, they may be bad. Their success or failure will be the greatest source of suffering or joy we are capable of experiencing. There is no pain greater than the loss of love, and sharper than the serpent's tooth is the ingratitude of a child or a lover for the intensely-focussed passion we have lavished on them. There is no greater joy than mutual love between adults, or between parents and children.

The third source of suffering lies in our struggle as a species to master this turbulent and dangerous world in which we have to live. More, we suffer in our struggle to change and improve it. Unlike other creatures on this planet, we have not been content to accept a fate that someone else has decided for us. We have challenged the gods, as Prometheus did when he stole fire from them to give to human beings. He was punished savagely and perhaps we all have to pay a price for daring to claim our dignity as human beings. From that has developed many marvels of creativity, heroism and imagination. The contradiction is that somewhere buried in those capacities we carry a peculiar fascination for inflicting pain and death on our own kind. It is the shadow that lies in all of us. None of us are free until we can recognize it in ourselves.

To begin to think about suffering brings one directly to religion. Its primary purpose has been to offer an explanation for the terrifying irrationality of the ills that afflict us. There is no religious leader who does not find it necessary to offer an explanation for physical, emotional and spiritual pain. Some of the rationalizations have been bizarre, some have been majestic, but there is a constant surge of human need to have the question of personal suffering given dignity through understanding and ritual. Tears have often played an important part in this process.

In the west our mainly secular society has affected views of what religion has to offer. Much of the institutional church has been rejected, but many people have retained the rituals of baptism, marriage and funerals, and recognize their deep significance. Birth, adults coming together to establish a private and secure unit, and death are sacramental experiences which seem to demand a public as well as a private commitment. All three are times when tears flow ... tears of joy, pleasure, pride and grief. Any society, including a secular society, will have to find ways of meeting these primary human responses in ways that acknowledge their significance.

But if suffering is universal, so too is the human drive to overcome it and seek happiness. It was this realization that brought me back to tears, because time and time again people said to me: 'It was only when I accepted and understood my tears that I began to pull myself out of despair'. I began to understand that there are different ways of crying. Some tears simply leave the person crying more exhausted and despairing. Others leave behind a feeling of coldness and detachment. But some experiences of crying are creative. The tears have a sense of purpose, of 'rightness'; they have a natural rhythm and a natural ending. The person crying is left relaxed and at peace. The emotion which triggered the tears has been acknowledged and let go.

Such crying is particularly important in bereavement. At a certain stage words cannot be found until tears come. At the inquest into the deaths of the Hungerford Massacre victims, the chairman of the bench, speaking in tribute to the clerk of the court who was among those killed, said, 'I find it impossible to put into words the shock felt in this court on a day like this. Perhaps we all find tears more appropriate.' A significant body of work has now built up in psychosomatic medicine to substantiate this intuitive understanding of the importance of tears.

That's not the whole story of course: some people dare not cry. It has been forbidden to them. Their awareness of suffering has been denied them, and sadly, with their capacity to know they suffer goes their capacity to know joy. The path to their joy may be through their tears.

The ability to know that we suffer, the ability to be aware of our joy is a peculiarly human attribute. In it lies our capacity to shape and plan our lives, to shape and plan our future and the future of the world in which we live. From this awareness we can learn to minimize unnecessary suffering and maximize joy for ourselves, and because we can do it for ourselves we can help others to do the same. It is when we cease to be aware; when that awareness has been taken away from us; when we have abandoned it; sold it for a mess of pottage or refused to claim it; that our humanity is threatened. Our tears are a fountain of renewal of the capacity to be aware of sorrow and joy on which we can constantly draw.

2
The Functions of Tears, Crying and Weeping

Cry-baby-cry
Punch him in the eye
Tie him to a lamp-post
And leave him there to die

Children's rhyme

THE VALUE OF TEARS

Crying and weeping have been used by humans of all ages, of all races, creeds and in all societies to express their deepest feelings. There are references to tears in the Bible, in the Koran, the Hindu Uphanishads and in every nation's folklore. The salt water used in the Jewish ceremony of Seder represents the tears that were shed by the Israelites when they were slaves in Egypt. Rain is often talked about as if it were tears from a god, or the sky weeping in compassion for the sorrows of the inhabitants of the earth. In stories from every country and every race of people, we find references to tears – tears of grief, tears of anger, tears of joy. Fairy tales from all cultures tell of the magic of tears. Crying is, primarily, a signal. It is the only one available to a small creature who needs care but who cannot yet talk, crawl, jump up and down, clutch or find any other way of engaging the attention of a responsible adult. What is interesting is why after six weeks of life it produces, not only noise, but tears. That lusty sound of crying is the basic way in which infants programmed to survive draw attention to the fact that all is not well with them. Desmond Morris suggests that the naked facial skin of the human species makes tear drops a powerful visual signal. All of us share that experience. What use are those cascades of water that some of us continue to produce for the rest of our lives ... sometimes to our embarrassment and shame, sometimes to our pleasure and relief?

Infants who can produce tears have a better chance of surviving.

11

Tearless crying, if it goes on for any length of time, can cause the soft, moist lining of the nose and throat to dry up. When this happens babies are more vulnerable to infection. So those who survived in the early days of the human race produced children who had the same built-in genetic advantage. We became a race of weepers, creatures who produce moisture which bathes our eyes – moisture which scientists have discovered is much more complex than anyone imagined.

In 1922 Alexander Fleming discovered that tears contain an anti-bacterial enzyme which prevents infection. Every time we blink, this is spread across the eye surface. About sixty tiny glands in the eyelid produce moisture, and when we get a bit of grit in our eye or anything else happens to irritate it, like cigarette smoke or onion smells, the main lacrimal gland produces a rush of tears to flush out the irritant, to prevent it damaging the eye and make it possible for us to see again.

In the 1980s we learned that the chemical composition of 'emotional' tears, that is tears stemming from feelings like grief, is different from tears stimulated by an irritant to the eye, like onions. There is still much to be learned, but it is already clear that some chemicals identified are part of the family of brain chemicals known as endorphines. These are thought to modulate pain sensation and stress-induced changes in the immune system. Tears seem to produce a kind of self-medication which eases states of tension.

Like so many of the miracles that keep our body functioning, we take our eyes and our tears for granted. We cry and weep in the lavatory, in our beds, in the cinema . . . women will weep into the pot of soup they're making. We cry at funerals, we weep at the beauty of a sunset, watching a film on television as the heroine dies or two people who have been separated are reunited.

When shedding these tears as a result of strong emotion, our bodies normally produce sounds and movements as an accompaniment. We tend to use the words crying and weeping inter-changeably but there can be subtle differences between them which express different stages of grief or joy. Crying is more often associated with a noisy attempt to communicate inner feeling, and in the case of grief an expression of anger and a rejection of the thought that has precipitated the tears. In weeping, the feeling is more often turned in, the communication is with oneself. Weeping often follows from crying. It can imply that the worst has happened: nothing more can be done.

CONFLICTS AROUND TEARS

There are many interesting questions to be asked. Since boy infants and girl infants cry equally, why is one sex given permission to continue to cry and another not? Why are some societies harsher than others in their refusal to allow men to cry? Some, like the North American Indians, will not allow children of either sex to cry. In China, even when a child is being punished and beaten for doing something wrong, the parent will whisper fiercely, 'You mustn't cry, you mustn't cry'. What's so wrong about crying, why is it so often seen as a sign of weakness? Why is this human ability not respected?

The sound is designed by nature to command attention; but that command may not suit the adults at that moment when they hear it. There may be enemies about and the sound of crying will attract them; or the parents may be engaged in urgent matters of their own. We know, again from research, that the sound of an infant crying can arouse very strong responses in the adult who has responsibility for that child. These can range from an immediate offer of help right through to murderous rage and anger. So crying, to serve its purpose, has to motivate help at a level which is not dangerous for either the child crying or the adult who hears the cry. It also has to achieve a solution to a variety of causes of distress. We know that most children use differing cries on differing wave lengths, which can identify whether the need is for food, comfort or contact. The last can be as urgent as the first two.

Tears and sound are only part of the story. The appearance of the face changes as the muscles adapt to the demands made by the flow of tears. The mouth opens to make breathing easier and the corners of the lip are pulled down. The eyebrows arch because the muscles round the eyes have to contract in order to protect them from the excessive blood pressure. It is the spasmodic pressure of the surface of the eye which activates the tear gland.

If the distress is urgent the whole body can be involved in the activity. The legs and arms will thrash about, the back arches, the total organism becomes involved in communicating the need for help. If this is delayed, a state of panic follows and the intensity of feeling seems to be such that it is experienced as a life-threatening experience. By now the child may no longer be able to recognize when help is offered, and will continue to scream in desperation even when comfort comes. If it does not come, exhaustion eventually takes over and the child will fall asleep, still sobbing.

The capacity to cry loud and long is an important survival mechanism. Children who are unable to do that are less likely to survive. 'The greetin' wean gets fed'. But distress and suffering do not stop in infancy. Nor, for most people, does the hope that someone will respond helpfully to a signal that help is needed.

Children in distress, before they learn to control themselves, will cry for as long as they can and as loudly as they can. Adults see their task as making their children cry as little as possible and as quietly as possible. They are normally very successful and most people learn, at quite an early age, to block tears and stop themselves crying except in very private situations. Some even learn never to cry.

CRYING WITHOUT KNOWING YOU'RE CRYING

The need to cry does not stop. Life does not stop and the tears go underground. Distress is suffered daily but few things are less common than seeing adults cry. We have to learn codes which enable us to continue to cry, but to do so in ways which will not distress, frighten or shock other people. We learn to cry like adults. The signal of distress has to be disguised and given a more acceptable face. The tears are held back, the noise is muted, but the message is unmistakeable to those who know how to interpret it.

Sitting in the dentist's chair we cannot weep, scream and shout as we would like to – not only because we have fingers and instruments in our mouth but because that kind of behaviour is forbidden. We have to content ourselves with the occasional wince or muted moan for which we immediately feel we must apologize. In other situations, some adults produce a brief yelp which would be heartrending if it were prolonged. Even in its brevity it may have an intensity of feeling which rouses anxiety in the hearer, but even this can be covered up with a swear word.

Some of us learn to bury our tears in our speech, controlling our facial muscles but communicating our distress through our tone of voice, rarely if ever sounding happy or contented. One example is the whiner, always plaintive and self-pitying, but often covering it up with a 'Look how brave I am' story. It is really a plea for love and protection. Another is the complainer, who often begins a sentence with, 'Have you heard', or 'Did you see', and a tone of outrage. The message is of anger, sometimes well-justified, but the tone a mixture of anger and distress. It is a controlled tantrum whose real trigger is earlier experiences of injustice which are constantly revived by current distress. It seeks not comfort, but confirmation that life is unjust.

In its most creative form the powerful energy of repressed tears can power pressure-groups or political activity. At its worst it can be a divisive force in organizations. The constant complainer cannot question the conviction on which he has based his life, cannot truly cooperate with anyone or give them hope and courage.

We can weep in distress, rage, even in joy if the intensity of stimulation is high enough. Sometimes the messages can be mixed. I watched an eleven-year-old girl child receiving a television award for the *Most Caring Child of the Year* because of the way, she, an only child whose father is dead, cares for a severely disabled mother. Seeing her burst into tears, described by the commentator as 'crying for joy', I wondered how much that child was weeping in sorrow for herself. The list of tasks she performed for her mother – taking her to the lavatory in the middle of the night, washing and dressing her, turning her over in bed – seemed an outrageous imposition which, even if the child did not recognize it as such, must be exhausting and diminishing of her childhood.

For some people, even the minimal use of sound to express distress is forbidden in the same way as tears are forbidden. The only way left to them to communicate feeling is through the muscles of their face. In a moment of sudden distress their faces will take on the classic shape of the distressed child – a turning-down of the corners of the mouth, the inner ends of the eyebrows raised so that they lie obliquely over the face, furrows in the forehead. This is the image of grief seen in masks throughout the world, the classic mask of tragedy, the face Munch painted in his portrait 'Shriek'. Each of us who deliberately puts our face into this shape will make contact with our own sadness just as making ourselves smile can bring about a sensation of cheerfulness.

For some people the classic shape of grief on their faces has become a chronic and habitual style. They go around the world with a frozen cry for all who choose to see. Unaware of their own sadness most of the time, they will recognize it only if their attention is drawn to it, and perhaps not even then.

There are others who show this response only when they are alone or not focussing on a specific task. In company, at work or in conversation, they are lively and animated. Alone or unoccupied, the mask of the frozen cry emerges ... the schoolchild who day-dreams, the secretary in pauses between dictation, the executive sitting on the lavatory. It is seen in public places where people may feel alone and anonymous although surrounded by others. Underground trains and public washrooms provide a perfect setting where the convention is that no one looks at anyone else. It can be particularly moving to see women come into the powder-room of a restaurant or ballroom where they have been wearing masks of hectic enjoyment and as the door between them and their party swings shut they let the mask of gaiety slide off and the frozen cry reveals itself.

Even feeling can be buried underground. In her novel *The Madness of a Seduced Woman*, Susan Fromberg Schaeffer describes the reaction of a woman at her mother's funeral.

And then I thought it was raining, and looked up in surprise, because we were in church, and even if it were raining, I should not be getting wet. I put my hand to my face and felt my cheeks, they were drenched and slippery. I looked down at the bodice of my dress and saw that drops of water had fallen onto it. When I touched the black poplin fabric, it was damp. Carefully, slowly, I raised my hand to my hair. My hair was dry. I didn't understand it. I looked out the window. The sun was shining. There wasn't a cloud anywhere. And with a shock I realized that I was crying and that I couldn't stop. It was as if my body and I had parted company and my body had decided to mourn my mother's death even if I had not.

Where all sounds of crying and all facial signs of distress have been excluded from the life-plan of the adult, the distress signals are driven underground. The messages which would have been sent to the face and vocal chords are sent to some other set of muscles.

When in pain, many people instead of crying will clench their fingers, or toes, their neck or calves or thighs. There is no part of the body which may not be used. In the dentist's chair we will squeeze its arms with both hands, we will tighten our stomach and diaphragm muscles or tightly curl our fingers and toes – anything rather than howl and sob as our instincts demand. Tensing ourselves in this way makes it possible for us to cry in our hands or feet or in our chest or gut, but not in our throat or face where it can be seen and where it is meant to happen. That would be seen to be 'childish'.

But not all pain is physical. Our distress can derive from fear, loneliness, grief or rage. If we have been denied permission to express those feelings in tears and sobs where do we express that pain? Certainly in our muscles – stiffening our necks, tightening our joints, tensing the muscles round our eyes. But also in our viscera – hardening our hearts, tightening our gut, with effects on health we do not fully understand. Our bodies armour themselves against feeling.

WAYS OF DISTRACTING OURSELVES FROM FEELINGS OF DISTRESS

If we are forced by the adults in our life to learn that crying is not acceptable, we can develop a number of 'tricks' to distract us from our distress. They act by producing a mildly disturbing sensation which interferes with the impulse to cry. Our capacity for consciousness is limited and by filling it with an alternative experience we can distract ourselves from the feeling we don't want to have. The alternative sensation doesn't need to be unpleasant – sucking a thumb, a blanket, later a cigarette. In some countries mothers or nursemaids will stroke a baby boy's genitals to soothe him.

Masturbation can become a diversion from distress for both girls and boys. Prisons and boarding schools are two settings where the comfort and distraction achieved by masturbation are much more important than the sexuality. Crying with homesickness can be seen or heard, rubbing the flesh to distract from the pain can be hidden more easily under the blankets. Violence can serve the same purpose by converting the pain of distress to anger either at oneself or at others. Self-mutilation, often found, for example, among adolescent girls in institutions who slash themselves with sharp instruments, is a seriously misunderstood alternative to weeping.

Other habits may be seen as minor forms of self-mutilation or distraction, such as nose-picking, ear-pulling, lip-biting, face-rubbing, nail-biting. Head-banging is a common response in children's nurseries where the little ones have learned that crying is a fairly hopeless or unproductive activity. It is, however, also one which has to be given up as the child grows up, but its power lingers in the description among delinquent youths of the most unhappy and disturbed member of their group as a 'headbanger'.

The essential strategy is to reduce the cry and the fear of crying by substituting a greater self-inflicted stimulation for a lesser which is passively suffered. The greater the distress, the more intense the necessary alternative. Self-mutilation by tattoos, drug-taking and heavy drinking are examples. The excitement of stealing reduces the tension for some, shopping for new clothes helps some women while many men find the absorption of gambling addictive. Attendance at Bingo halls can become compulsive for women.

Most have learned that if we are under attack, weeping or crying makes us more vulnerable. Women can use this to emphasise their vulnerability, arouse pity and in that way get themselves out of a dangerous situation. Most men are not permitted to use tears in this way. Only when a man accepts an honourable defeat or when he has triumphed is a show of weakness tolerated. Tears after triumph or defeat in the boxing ring, on the athletic track or the football field may express triumph or relief at survival, or act as a relief from tension. But even here crying may be seen as a dangerous weakness and a laugh or a joke substituted.

Jewish humour has brought this to a fine art. Few peoples have had more cause for tears and none have a richer fund of black humour where pain is managed and contained so that privacy and dignity may be maintained. Two young Jewish women watched their families being led to the gas chamber while they themselves were taken to be stripped and shaved. They told me that on first encountering each other naked and bald, they fell into each other's arms, unable to speak for laughing. Their terror and pain were too intolerable to be expressed in any other way.

Law courts provide many examples of the refusal of young men to admit their emotional vulnerability. They display the bravado of laughter when they may be near to tears. If sentenced to prison, while their mothers may be rending the air of the courtroom with screams of protestations, the offenders will smile broadly. The jury seeing the smile will take it as an affirmation of villainy. Few will recognize it as a defence against tears which would 'unman' them.

THE ALTERNATIVE OF ANGER

In a small child, the tantrum, that marvellous pyrotechnic display of naked feeling, involves the whole being. It comes into play when to express distress through words or tears seems pointless and there is enough energy available for rage. It is a healthier reaction than falling asleep in despair, but not easy for adults to cope with. Those people who in adult life continue to claim the right to explode directly from distress to anger will often find themselves in prison or mental hospital. Some men and women exploit their marriages to provide opportunities, in a private arena, to re-enact that early drama.

But there are also children who are never allowed to explode into ordinary anger, who never have the opportunity to experience and understand themselves in that way. They go through their childhood 'grizzling', trapped in a bleak world between anger and tears. Such people may spend their adult lives permanently irritable, or with small uncontrolled explosions of anger when they face minor causes of distress. Such people have not learned a comfortable way of responding to their own implicit distress cry. They make uncomfortable colleagues and are a menace behind the wheel of a car. If something happens to inhibit the anger or interfere with it, if for example someone is unexpectedly kind to them, they suddenly find themselves with a strong impulse to cry. Tears and anger become two faces of the same coin, feelings swivelling between one and the other.

Healthy crying and healthy anger are the right of every child and every adult. Boy children are likely to be taught that they mustn't cry and girl children that they mustn't be angry. Anger becomes, for men, a one-sided way of showing feeling; tears are often used by women in situations where anger would be more appropriate. Because there is no room for manoeuvre, each can be used in negative ways.

Righteous anger is glorious to watch and to experience. But anger that is blind in its denial of the tears it masks in the angry person, that falls over the border into violence against whoever or whatever is in its path, is usually destructive. It is rarely about the apparent object of its wrath, much more likely to be powered from roots deep in the individual's past before tears were banned as a way of showing distress. Violence within the family often lies here.

We are left with a basic question. Given that we are human, given that to be human involves a range of feelings which include suffering and unavoidable distress – as well as moments of unutterable bliss – how may a human person cry without being heard or seen? That seems to be what our society is trying to achieve. If it can be done, then what is the price we have to pay and is it worth it? We should also ask ourselves whose needs are served by these restraints on our expressions of distress.

PARENTAL ATTITUDES TO CRYING

On the day my mind stopped breathing
I was only four years old
It was then I started learning
to do what I was told.
My world should have gotten bigger
but it's gotten very small.
If my mind's not breathing soon again
I'll have no world at all.

Edward Matchett, *Journeys of Nothing in the Land of Everything.*

Parents hate to hear their children cry. The sound of crying is within the spectrum of the greatest sensitivity of the human ear. It needs to be. Each child's survival depends totally on having an adult close who will protect her, feed her, keep her warm and safe. In return for this attention, there are few experiences which are more satisfying than to soothe a distressed child and see the relaxation and contentment that follows.

In his short story, *NOCTURNE one*, Carl MacDougall describes how a writer, working through the night, hears his son crying and goes to comfort him:

He is standing, holding onto the cot rails, trampolining up and down to the rhythm of his sobs. He sees you and cries louder . . .

so you pick him up, and immediately you lean forward to grab him under the arms he stops crying. He stops crying and rests a soft teary cheek on your lips and something is born inside as you kiss the wee face. And when a memory jolt of his bad dream flings his head back, he gets ready to bawl, but instead of crying he smiles and replaces, snuggles, his cheek beside your mouth to be kissed again. And you kiss it again.

But equally there are few more frustrating experiences than failing to pacify a distressed child. If the cry goes on and on despite one's best efforts, it arouses sensations ranging from despair and helplessness to murderous rage.

As a defence, most adults who encounter children in intimate situations develop a set of attitudes and responses to help them cope. They develop a personal philosophy that gives them a framework to understand what crying is about and what it entitles the child to in the way of attention. Either from this or from their own earlier experiences of being a crying child (which all of us have been) attitudes and feelings about the public display of grief, distress and suffering evolve.

Stone age babies, twentieth-century parents

Each of us, whether born in a high flat in Glasgow, a penthouse in the Barbican or a mud hut in a jungle has to conform to the social rules of living in that community. Our willingness to obey the rules can only be taught to us through love or fear of the adults caring for us. Each of us has been through this process of learning what is considered tolerable or intolerable behaviour. By and large we hold on to this mental structure for most of our lives, shifting our attitudes only when a majority of our fellow citizens shift theirs. We use roughly the same ways of communicating our ideas of how to behave and how not to behave to our children, as were used for us.

Exactly how this is done is decided in ways that bear little relationship to the primary needs of the children but much to the economic network in which the family functions. Melvin Konner studied the !Kung society, where the simplicity of the life made it natural for babies in the first year of their lives never to be out of their mother's sight, if not her arms. He suggests that in highly-developed, wealthy economies there is no biological advantage for the child to be cared for by one parent as opposed to being cared for equally by two, and sees no reason why this marvellous experience should be reserved for women. In some countries the idea of both parents taking responsibility for child care is being seen as an ideal to be achieved and paternity leave is now being claimed as well as maternity leave.

But the more common pattern is still that the mother (or a female carer if the mother is working) will have the early responsibility for teaching behaviour, with father sharing responsibility when the child begins to be physically more independent, mobile, verbal and capable of feeding itself. Even so, the behaviour taught by the women will be determined by what men think is right. Girls will be brought up differently from boys. Girls are more likely to be given the right to weep, to complain, to make a fuss, to declare their pain and unhappiness. Boys will be prepared for the world of competitiveness, material achievement and endurance of suffering. Their distress will be dealt with quite differently.

Konner tells us how the !Kung mother and child, living in total interdependence for the first year, deal with the child's distress. The nipple is always available to the baby. His research showed that there was only an average of six seconds between an infant beginning to be fretful and the mother responding. The mother is, of course, with the infant twenty-four hours a day – an idea which would fill most mothers in the 'advanced' world with horror.

Such a regime is in stark contradiction to the highly individualistic society in which Europeans and Americans live, where parents claim their rights to space, freedom and privacy even during the infancy of their children. Those who can will return to work in the world of male values, and delegate the most intimate tasks of parenting to other young women, most of whom have failed to achieve the educational and social status which would have enabled them to avoid child care. They will be unlikely to give the intense attention necessary to minimize infant distress.

Few parents can afford a trained nanny who would expect, in addition to caring for the baby, to have someone else to do the washing, ironing and general cleaning. Untrained carers are often expected to do all these things as well as care for the baby. It is not surprising if the baby's distress is ignored or smothered with sugary foods. What is surprising is that more babies are not damaged by amateur carers.

When there are two small children the stress on a carer is even greater. Walking invisibly into many a small suburban semi that the mother has left with such a rush in the morning, one can find an eighteen-year-old carrying a baby on one arm, wielding a Hoover with the other, followed by a grizzling toddler. Many children will have a six-monthly or yearly succession of these 'carers', most of whom are still struggling with their own problems of growing up.

Where the parent has no alternative but to work and use public child-care services, it can be even less likely that the child will have the individual attention that ensures a comfortable infancy. The staff are frequently under stress, particularly in inner-city areas, and their training seldom equips them to cope with the handling of tears, crying and distress. Like parents, they use their own rough-and-ready philosophy.

In the industrial world, the sound of a child crying – left for example in a pram outside a shop and emitting heart-breaking screams of distress – raises little comment. But in a world of early rising for work, small houses with indifferent sound insulation, the howl of an infant during the night, or even during the day, ceases to be a private matter between the child and its carer. In a world uncertain about the nature of caring and the nature of loving, it signals irritation on the part of the neighbours and failure on the part of the parent. In adults uncertain of their own capacity to claim attention and care it rouses memories of their own unsatisfied needs. So now being forced to relive this part of their own past history the carer is faced with a choice: either to repeat with the child the same techniques that were used by their own parents, to hit or frighten them into silence, or to treat the cry of the child as they would have wanted to be treated, had they been given an informed choice.

In the !Kung world the sound of crying is hardly an issue in normal day to day encounters. When it does occur it will be in the context of serious distress and therefore will have meaning and be shown respect within the group: also there are no memories buried deep within the psyche of unrewarded and neglected screams of distress to be reactivated in the adults of the community. The encounter with the suffering child will be uncluttered by ghosts of one's own pain.

It requires a remarkable degree of insight to break the patterns we were offered by our own parents. If the solution to unacceptable behaviour was to be hit, then 'It never did *me* any harm', is another way of saying, 'My parents could do no wrong, I must have been bad if they hit me. I must have deserved it'. The person who says that is unable to separate their own judgement from that of their parents and can only follow docilely in their footsteps. Loving and helpful responses to similar situations would give the next generation of parents encouragement to offer the same.

Patterns of response to crying

From these springs, the individual philosophy develops. We can either accept the validity of tears and crying as a respectable human activity, or reject it as shameful, humiliating, embarrassing behaviour. The first tries to discover the source of the distress, remove it and comfort and console the child. The second tends to punish and discourage crying in children.

Many people are torn between the two and, depending on the pressures of the moment, will comfort or punish. Most work out a rough system for punishing or soothing which fits into their capacity to sympathize. Children soon learn to negotiate a maze which may be quite incomprehensible to an outsider, based as it is on the private experience of the parent. An infant may be allowed to cry but a toddler will be punished. Sympathy may be given to a child who cries because he has fallen and hurt himself but fury may be aroused if he touches something that breaks. Crying inside the house may be tolerated but not crying in public, gentle sobs may be more acceptable than howls of rage or vice-versa. Some parents can accept any form of tears except those which appear to criticize their own behaviour.

Crying is one of a range of basic human reactions that get children into trouble. Sylvan Tomkins in his book *Affect Imagery Consciousness* identified curiosity that leads them to explore the world; hurting themselves because they try to do things they haven't yet acquired the skills to do safely; wanting to be with the adult whom they love; wanting to copy and share what the adults they love are doing; being joyful and noisy; being shy; showing fear. These experiences form the basis of an open, balanced and creative life, but all of them can be crushed or distorted.

We should never forget how dependent children are on their parents' approval, how much they want to please them, how much they will adapt their behaviour to please them, even tolerating pain, anxiety, and humiliation. Only when they have failed time after time to attract love, will they give up. So it is possible for even the most powerful drive like the need to cry to be muted, driven underground, destroyed. Offending behaviour can be punished by shame, terror, pain, blackmail, the threat of withdrawal of love or indifference.

Shaming or ridicule is perhaps the most common. 'Big boys don't cry. Cry baby'. Or the more straightforward 'You should be ashamed of making a fool of yourself like that'. This technique is only effective when the child is old enough to have some idea of self, and some idea of the kind of person their carer or parent wants them to be. The attack can embed itself deeply into the consciousness of the child, so that he or she will continue to use it to monitor their own behaviour.

Terrorizing a child is also a remarkably common form of behaviour. We can watch it in department stores, at bus stops, in queues. I last saw it in a public lavatory. The child is crying at any level from outright howling to grizzling. The parent is trying to ignore it but the thread breaks and suddenly the child is pounced on, shaken viciously and shouted or hissed at in the most terrifying way: 'Stop it!' with an additional phrase thrown in like, 'if you don't stop that crying I'll really give you something to cry for'. Or as I heard one mother say to twins, both of whom were crying: 'If you don't stop, I'll give one of you away, now which will it be?' The child freezes and the crying stops. A resilient child will start again within a few minutes after the shock has worn off which will lead to another technique being applied – probably pain.

Pain is the crudest response but, although as morally repulsive, probably least damaging in the long term if it is restricted to a slap. But human beings have widely varying levels of control, and the physical punishment can escalate until it becomes cruelty – sometimes even murder. For that reason society is learning, slowly but surely, that the infliction of physical pain on children, even in the form of a slap, can no longer be tolerated. We have no idea how many cases of child abuse have been triggered by a child crying for comfort which the parent isn't able to give. It certainly comes up time after time in social work case histories as an offered justification for the cruelty inflicted. It is even offered as a defence in child murder. 'He just kept on crying and I couldn't stand it any longer' is a stock excuse. And it has validity. In this case the adult has, inside his head become a distressed child himself and has had the adult equivalent of a crying tantrum – an explosion of rage – with fatal results.

Blackmail. In adults, blackmail is considered one of the most unattractive crimes, playing as it does on intimidation and abuse of power. Yet it is constantly used to control children. 'You'll make mummy cry if you don't stop crying'. 'You'll be the death of me with your crying, stop it, I can't stand it'. The child is put in touch with her capacity to destroy and made to fear it rather than learn to control it. If she responds honestly to her need to cry, she is told she will damage the person on whom she relies for affection and care. It is not a real choice. A false morality is invoked: the crying child becomes a 'bad' child and the non-crying child a 'good' child.

Threats of withdrawal of love are common currency. 'Mummy won't love you if you don't stop crying'. 'I don't like little girls/boys who cry'. What horrors are opened up with these sentences: the implication that love is dependent on acceptable behaviour; the notion that it can be switched off like a light. What a message with which to send the small child stumbling on her way into the world of relationships. Or the demonstration of it given in the ultimate punishment of the appearance of indifference.

A show of indifference to the child's feelings. In this method the parent or carer does nothing other than turn away or leave the room or not go to where the child is when the crying begins. No action is taken to comfort or soothe. The child is simply allowed to cry itself out. This can last for a few minutes or for several hours until the child falls asleep from exhaustion. Sometimes the indifference is real, not just a show. I watched recently a commercial creche operating in a gymnasium where mothers left their children while they practised aerobics. A seated infant cried unremittingly while the woman in charge laboriously went about a series of routine chores. She had acquired immunity to sounds of distress, and was puzzled when I intervened. If these messages are consistently repeated the child learns that there is no use asking for help because none will be given. It is interesting that a consistent theme in fairy tales, like Cinderella, is that tears can be a signal for a helper to appear.

Another pattern is to offer practical help without sympathy. Busy nursery staff may be tempted to use phrases like, 'That's enough of that, let's see what's the matter', as the infant is efficiently checked over, changed and redressed . . . and then left to cry. Other pressures may lead to sympathy being offered without practical help though this response is more likely to be aroused in men who feel helpless when faced with a small child. As in so many other situations an adult who feels helpless is the most dangerous partner a child is likely to encounter, but in either situation, help without sympathy or sympathy without help, the child is deprived of a vital learning experience of how we put feelings and behaviour together, or else is taught the damaging lesson that they don't go together. Help without sympathy, as some hospital patients asking for a bed pan will tell you, can be experienced as a hostile act.

For children, help without sympathy, duty rather than love, denies the emotional component of the tears and the feelings that go with them. This is sometimes put into words – 'Crying won't get you anywhere'. 'If you just keep on crying, you'll *never* be able to do anything about it'.

A cheerful, jollying response is common where the parent or carer decides that the cause of distress and the cry that has gone with it are trivial and can be dealt with by laughter. In a total experience of crying which has been treated with respect this can be an occasionally useful and undamaging response. As a constant way of dealing with distress, pain or fear it has nothing to recommend it, leading as it does to shame and ultimately denial. To be laughed at rather than with is not an experience most people enjoy – particularly when they are seeking comfort.

Jean Liedloff, in her book *The Continuum Concept*, argues that many personal problems and most social ills are caused by the way we bring up our children in the 'advanced' countries. She too lived with a 'primitive' tribe and watched how they cared for their infants. She argues that the human embryo is programmed to expect certain responses from the outside world. One of the earliest expectations is for constant contact with its mother's skin and body for the first months of life, probably until it is independently mobile, and then for significant periods of time after that when the child feels the need. Deprivation of this experience she describes as a kind of torture.

She believes that the vast majority of parents love their children deeply and have no idea of the suffering they are causing or the agony of the baby left alone to weep in its cot. We seem to need words spoken or written before we take messages seriously. Body language has less command over us, but that is all a baby has to offer. Babies cannot put words to their complaints, they cannot appeal to an authority. Even more, they cannot link their pain and distress at being left alone to the cause of it and, if not abandoned for too long, they greet their parents with joy when they return.

What she fails to do is to acknowledge the fact that it is precisely the human capacity to stand back and question the meaning of life that presents the dilemmas. It is the human capacity for choice that tears us apart from our stone-age babies. If the !Kung tribe of Konner or the Yequana of Liedloff were suddenly transported to New York, in two generations they would have abandoned their current child-rearing practices and reproduce the same problems that we have. Give women anywhere opportunities for stimulation and the wider scope available to men and they will take them.

Part of our survival capacity as a race is that we have a compulsion to reach out to new ideas, and to try new things. It is always the people who have had lots of opportunities to taste and explore the world who are happy to go back to simpler ways of living. It is the hungry and exploited adults of the world who leave societies which have these emotional benefits for children to try to make a better life for themselves in the economically advanced countries. Our problem is how to help our stone-age babies survive the emotional deprivation of the world we are creating. We can save their lives but how can we preserve their sanity? How can we call a truce?

Only parents can do that but they need to have the help and support of the whole community. Those whose own children have grown up can reassure younger parents that even the most inconsolably demanding infants will stop squalling in their own good time. With loving acceptance and security that will happen sooner rather than later. We all need to recognize the anxieties and conflicts facing young parents – their fears about what the neigh-bours, their mothers-in-law, the other people in the restaurant, will say. By helping and supporting them we make life easier for their babies as well. Sources of conflict and anxiety should wherever possible be eliminated. Many of them are built into our way of life. Shops, hotels, restaurants, trains and buses are designed for adults without children. They should be reorganized to honour parents with babies, not discriminate against them. Most of all, each of us needs to honour the infant we once were.

In today's world many young parents are facing intolerable conflicts. I met one young mother changing her baby's nappy in a public washroom. He was gurgling and laughing up at her and I expressed my delight and admiration of him. To my dismay she burst into tears, saying that she had only another week at home with him because she had to go back to work to help pay the mortgage.

Other mothers may choose to go back to work convinced that they will be better and more loving mothers on a part-time basis. Some mothers may prefer to reduce their standard of living and stay home.

But wherever babies are in alternative care they are entitled to a quality of service which is responsive to their emotional as well as their physical needs.

Modifying conflict

Adults have an awesome power over children. An infant life is totally dependent on the person caring for it being willing to respond to its needs for food and shelter. In the same way it is dependent on an adult being willing to respond to less obvious but equally important needs for skin contact and stimulation. A baby fed and kept warm and clean by a machine would not grow up to be a human being with abilities to talk, live and love.

If a child's need is given priority by a carer, help or comfort will be offered immediately. Distress will be kept at a minimum. At the beginning of our lives we only have needs. Wants develop later when we begin to have a sense of ourselves as a person and have choice. The child's hungers for food, comfort and stimulation are needs. She has no choice. In affluent societies there is seldom a conflict of needs between a child and the parent, but there is often a conflict between the child's needs and the parents' wants. It is here that the dilemma lies.

An infant's needs are out of its control. Understanding this leads to a search for the cause of the problem and an attempt to remedy it. The nature of the cry offers a clue. Research suggests that some mothers learn to distinguish between the sounds of these cries, that they have differing wave-lengths depending whether the source lies in hunger, discomfort or the need for attention.

The child would normally be picked up, held, patted, looked at, talked to, smiled at, soothed, while being fed or changed. The non-verbal messages coming from the adult to the child will depend on the carer's confidence and relaxation. My own daughter cried unremittingly in infancy when we visited my mother-in-law, whom I felt was always poised to criticize me. If the crying continues when the cause has passed, it can often be stopped by distracting the child with sharp sounds or visual effects. The most modern babies are being soothed with a tape recording of the mother's heartbeats to which they became accustomed in the womb. Standing or walking with the child is also more soothing than sitting down with it because that more closely resembles the womb-like experience. Older children can be reassured with words or familiar endearments.

A group of infants and mothers were watched in their own homes during the first year of life to see if an immediate response to crying made any difference. They found that mothers who persistently ignored crying during the first few months of life tended to have babies who cried increasingly over the remainder of the first year. Prompt comfort led to a reduction in the amount of crying. These babies also had the best communication skills between eight and twelve months. The conclusion was that prompt care-giving, if it also involves paying attention to the baby's social as well as physical state, is best for both mother and baby.

But it would be a mistake to think that it is simple for all parents to offer this quality of care. A particular problem exists for that group of parents, ordinary, potentially loving parents with children who cry constantly from birth. In the first weeks of life crying scores for babies range from ten to 190 minutes a day. Caring for an excessively crying baby has been compared to sleep deprivation torture, and while the problem lasts the parents can take little pleasure in the child. They drag through their days in a state of exhaustion and the relationship between the parents themselves also suffers, sometimes irrevocably. Fears of harming the child are very common among such parents and sometimes this actually happens. The miracle is that it doesn't happen more often.

There are some children who simply seem to have missed out on the ability to differentiate the sounds they make, and the parents are therefore deprived of the power to respond relevantly. The parent cannot recognize the signals and is normally flooded with guilt and anxiety as a result. With some children there is no identifiable reason for this and as other skills of communication, like language, develop, difficulties abate, although parents can be left with a lifetime sense of failure about their response to their child's early crying. We all have a great need to make sense of the signals surrounding us and the tension of frustration and anxiety which results can very easily be communicated to the child.

John Kirkland's book *Crying and Babies* makes an honest attempt to help the parents of crying babies cope, but although he offers a range of possibilities of causes of crying, nutritional (including maternal allergies), medical and psychiatric, at the end of the book the phenomenon remains a mystery. On the basis of his research he offers several helpful programmes for parents and voluntary helpers. These help them primarily to 'see' their child through the haze of anger, exhaustion and guilt which so often accompany baby crying. Letters sent to Kirkland often refer to their babies having been separated from them in hospital and not having settled after that. A cycle of tension seems to be set up which takes a long time to repair. Relaxed babies don't cry. Inexperienced or tired mothers try to manage mostly by leaving and or ignoring their crying restless babies. Some parents are inhibited and shy with their babies, being too embarrassed to talk to them or sing to them. It's as if they fear their child's critical capacity as they once doubted their own acceptability. The actual amount of crying doesn't seem to be relevant. What matters is the parent's perception of what is going on.

A constantly crying child, coupled with sleep loss, fatigue, loneliness and a sense of failure inevitably exposes the cracks in all the other domestic arrangements, including the marriage. Parents can experience for the first time in their lives their own capacity for going beyond the boundaries of what they have always seen as reasonable behaviour. Relationships with the crying child can be shadowed for years with the memories of barely restrained murderous impulses against the child for whom, in their innocence, they assumed they would feel only love. Parents of inconsolable babies can be as scarred as their children since in the first few weeks after birth most parents respond to crying with an urge to care and protect. The continuous crying can be interpreted as cruel rejection. John Kirkland only recommends letting the child 'cry it out' if staying with the child would endanger its life. There is a point at which the parents realize they might be driven to kill the baby to keep it quiet.

Parents who severely batter a child, sometimes to death, frequently try to justify their actions by saying that the child was deliberately crying in order to provoke them. There is no doubt that they believe this, even of a baby only a few months old. Lewis Carroll made the point,

> *Speak roughly to your little boy*
> *And beat him when he sneezes*
> *He only does it to annoy*
> *Because he knows it teases*

Parents who believe that of infants usually have no ability to distinguish between needs and wants in their own lives, any more than they can for their children. They cannot see the child as a person in its own right rather than as an extension of themselves. It may be that no one responded to their infant cries for help.

A child can be seen as one's own parent nagging, nagging, nagging. She can be the young sister whose cries took mother's attention away from us. He can be the younger brother whose birth was doubly welcomed because he was a boy, or because he had red hair, blue eyes - any one of a number of things. For fathers, the child can be the rival they always feared, who pushes them out of first place in their wife's arms. For mothers, the child can represent the dependency they were never allowed to enjoy so can't offer to anyone else. Memories, conscious and unconscious, mean that this relationship can never be pure, can never be free of the parent's own early experience. All we can hope for is to understand and where it is appropriate to break the chain.

Part of the strain is caused by the fact that parenthood is often sentimentalized and the child is expected to fit smoothly into the pattern of an egalitarian marriage where the couple expect to continue to spend their evenings and weekends together free of interference by the children. The notion that a successful mother 'puts the child down' at seven p.m. and the couple are undisturbed until seven a.m. is very destructive to a realistic understanding of a child's role in the family. If that doesn't succeed, if the child refuses to sleep and cries constantly, it is also very destructive to the mother's self-image, since she feels she is failing both the baby and her husband's expectations of her.

Many women are still trapped in the image of themselves as the ideal mother-figure and are often reluctant to cast off their husband's expectation that she will be his mother as well as the baby's. The solution of letting the baby stay up, of letting it sleep with the parents and for the parents to readjust their sleeping patterns to the child's is difficult, alien and feels like 'giving in' to the child. Yet it may be the right one.

It has been found that in babies, sleep patterns often involve waking many times and surfacing into light sleep and at this point they may seek contact or food before falling asleep again. If these are not immediately available, crying will follow the wakening. This pattern may have had profound survival-value for our species since an infant sleeping alone in early societies would be at great risk from prowling animals.

Here again we meet misunderstanding of the difference between what the child needs and what the child wants. Parents have often a great fear of 'spoiling' a baby as if he is a piece of fruit that will go 'off'. Underlying this seems to be a fear that the child is a monster in disguise who if given the chance will devour them and take away their freedom. The cartoonist Heath has amused us for years with images of huge infants terrorizing their parents. It may be the greedy and devouring baby we once were who is coming back to life in these thoughts.

A particularly powerful fantasy is that a baby will try to manipulate adults with its crying. Generations of baby books, mostly written by men, have warned mothers about this and emphasized the need to resist the infant's machinations. To exhausted parents this must be a very tempting view. It relieves their guilt and gives them legitimacy for behaving in ways that they would in a more normal frame of mind condemn as cruel.

It is not surprising that parents in distress but anxious to do the best for their child have turned to authority figures to advise them. The growth of professionalism, as well as saving babies' lives eroded many parents' confidence in their natural wisdom. This is gradually being restored as the importance of partnership and sharing of power between professionals and lay people is becoming more clearly understood and valued. Advice in the past for parents of crying babies was not always good and even to-day advice columns may be read which recommend parents to 'declare war', in Jill Liedloff's phrase, by letting their baby 'cry it out'. Happily, in the main, advice is improving. Part of the problem is the cult of independence that makes young couples think they ought to be able to manage on their own. Very few can. The most effective self-help group for parents of constantly crying children has been CRY-SIS which has an emergency help line and a support network. Their stories of desperate parents make painful reading.

What is needed to help all families with small children, particularly where there is a constantly crying baby, no matter the cause, is massive support for the parents from family, friends and neighbours: in other words, from the community. Child-care may need to be taken in shifts to enable the parents to get enough sleep. Help should be mobilized to clean the house, cook meals, do the laundry and care for older children, just as would happen if the baby were ill or severely disabled in some way. This is one problem we know will pass as the child grows and we should be prepared to help parents during the months it will take. Their children are our future.

*   *   *

Humans belong to the group of animals which cling, follow closely and protest loudly when left alone. In early groups of humans no baby would ever be left alone. It's worth remembering the !Kung babies for whom the mother is always available. Perhaps we can't expect Western women to behave like stone-age mothers, but we could try to remember that babies have no choice about being stone-age babies. They know nothing about status, careers, romantic love and all the other baggage adults carry around. What they respond to is what Jill Hoffman describes herself as responding to in her gut-tearing poem, 'Rendezvous', when her child cries in the night and she leaves her bed to answer the call – 'We meet, couple, and cling, in the dim light – / . . .' She describes the baby's 'brimming face' 'where milky drops glide' / 'I see my body's pleasure flood and yawn . . . It is a poem which excludes fathers, but it describes better than any other I know, that primary love affair, the continuation of the relationship within the womb until the young creature can cope a little bit more independently in the world outside the mother, a world in which we all ultimately make our way alone.

SOME WAYS IN WHICH ADULTS MAY BE AFFECTED BY THEIR EARLY EXPERIENCES OF DISTRESS

'Wake up', said a voice when I was three
'There's a great big world you must go and see'
'Wake up', said a voice when I was eight
'There's a better world you can help create'
'Wake up', said a voice when I was ten
'Or else your egg will be hard again'
'Wake up', said a voice at twenty-nine
'You've a lovely wife called Caroline'
'Wake up', said a voice at fifty-four
But the cuckoo
was frozen
behind its door.

Edward Matchett, *Journeys of Nothing in the Land of Everything.*

No one can say if any particular experience in childhood will or will not have damaging consequences. We do not hear enough of the healthy survivors of awful childhood experiences or really know a great deal about the mechanics of survival. What we do know is that many people seem to have an extraordinary capacity to adjust, to survive and to heal themselves. The effects of any experience, no matter how damaging it appears – abandonment, sexual abuse, all kinds of cruelty – will always depend on other factors in our lives. It depends essentially on the total life experience within which the awful thing happened. When we replay the experience in our memory or when talking and thinking about it, we are constantly changing its meaning for ourselves so there is always hope.

Early experience can be retrieved and transformed, sometimes by ourselves, sometimes with the help of other people. It can also be used creatively. It is only when we close the discussion by saying, 'I'm a failure', 'I'm useless', 'I'm a bad person', and no longer question those labels, that our capacity for change is truly diminished. But how a small child learns to deal with her first experiences of distress, how she is responded to when she asks for help in the simple demands of being fed, kept warm, dry and secure, is critical in determining her ability to respond in later, difficult encounters with the world.

Links between distress and punishment

If in a shop or in the street, we watch a toddler being punished for crying, perhaps by an exhausted young mother trying to cope with an infant as well as the toddler, or by an embarrassed father, the first thing we notice is that the child screams louder than ever. The distress increases for the child. The child regularly punished for crying, either by a blow, or rejection or by the failure of the adult to come to her aid, is doubly punished as against the child who is immediately comforted. In later life, such a child will automatically exaggerate any distress or injury.

This is particularly so for children who are punished for crying when they are hurt. The father or mother who does this, intent on producing a physically brave grown-up, is likely to produce just the opposite. In the adult, pain or the possibility of pain, serious injury or illness will reactivate the memory of more severe distress than would have been the case had the original experiences of pain been treated in a soothing way. Such an adult can exaggerate his suffering – and fear will be added to the combination of pain and distress.

The normal human response to pain is a cry of distress. If this is inhibited by fear of disapproval, the fear will increase and the combination can lead to panic. Men and women being trained to resist torture are taught not to be ashamed or embarrassed about shouting, screaming and displaying the fact that they are suffering. To do that actually increases their resistance to pain.

Women are thought to be more able than men to cope with pain: if so, perhaps this is because they have, in the past, been allowed to cry out and weep. Many women see their men as making an inordinate fuss over any injury or illness, but it may be that for these men the innate cry of pain has in their past become linked to the idea of more pain and punishment. If they have avoided a frozen face or a stiff upper lip they may nevertheless whimper at any small pain in the remembered expectation that it will get worse.

Links between fear and distress

The combination of fear and distress can lower our ability to tolerate frustration. If a toddler's problem cannot be solved immediately or she is deprived of something she wants, that evokes distress. To have a tantrum, which is a mixture of crying and anger, is a normal response at that stage of development. The toddler is caught between the crying of the helpless infant and the energy-filled urge for self-determination of the growing personality. But some children who have a tantrum may be shaken into terror by an irate adult. Where fear becomes deeply linked to distress, the adult who has been constantly exposed to this combination may find himself with a weakened ability to tolerate problems and frustration. The combined burden is too great. A toddler's tantrum can be coped with: an adult explosion of weeping and rage is a very different matter. The husband whose football team is beaten on Saturday afternoon is distressed but if he has also invested his identity and status in his team, which is what happens with some men, the threat to his self-esteem is such that after drinking heavily on Saturday night he will go home and beat up his wife. The same response can occur if a wife is reluctant to share in sexual activity. The frustration can ally itself with fear of rejection and a full-blown explosion with violence and rape can result. So too with encounters between fathers and children. Any situation of disobedience on the part of the child which leaves the father feeling helpless and afraid of losing his authority may be dealt with by an explosion of rage, even if the child is an infant who is only refusing to eat her food.

People for whom fear and distress are linked together in childhood have particular difficulties in tolerating the loss of love in adult life. Yet this ability is necessary if we are ever to achieve a firm sense of ourselves as individuals who are not utterly dependent on others for approval. Loneliness and a sense of being different are unpleasant for most people, but tolerable if they are not associated with fear, then they become terrifying. The child who has been made to feel fear whenever she feels like crying is particularly vulnerable to the threat of separation from the parent who produced the fear/distress link. Some parents spell this out to a crying child, even saying, 'I'll go away and leave you if you don't stop that noise'. Such experiences can lead to extremes of submissiveness in adults but can also in adolescence be the source of outrageous rebellion.

Such people can be made very anxious simply by seeing distress in other people. Women describe experiences of telling husbands that they are not feeling well or that they are tired, only to be met with a barrage of complaints from the husband about his own state of health and fatigue. The wives are seeking sympathy but what they trigger off in their husbands is fear: this is the reason for their response, not lack of sympathetic imagination. Those whose own need for comfort as children was not met cannot easily offer comfort to anyone else. One husband with a wife suffering from a progressive paralysis denied her need for care so effectively that he refused to change his very heavy manual gear car or move from a totally unsuitable house, even when it was obvious that she could no longer cope. Another, after an operation for breast cancer, had to conceal from her husband that she was still attending the hospital for follow-up radium therapy. To avoid his anger she would make up her face to look healthy no matter how ill she felt.

Heavy doses of undischarged fear are actually dangerous for the body, but because it is unacceptable for adults to show fear, we erect defences against it. The most common defence is to behave in the opposite way to that which we really feel. People who use this defence live always in the best of all possible worlds, where tiredness, sickness and failure are denied. To maintain this image they will either work compulsively or avoid confronting problems, leaving them to other people to deal with.

To punish a child's tears of distress faces the child with the problem of how to cry without being seen or heard. This can be learnt but it creates an additional problem of coping with the fear of showing distress which can be more devastating than the distress itself.

Shame and distress

Everything that happens when we link fear and distress can also happen when we link shame and distress. Ordinary human experiences of sickness or fatigue, difficulties in problem-solving, threats of loss of love, any occasion of loneliness . . . these become doubly difficult to tolerate when shame is added to distress by the parent who tells us that crying is cowardly, disgusting, babyish. The child who was taught to hang her head in shame because she felt like crying, as an adult is constantly apologizing for her existence, heaping contempt upon herself when faced with any distressing experience. On the other hand she may claim that there is really never any reason to get distressed and in order to minimize distress manages to avoid taking emotional, physical or social risks. For some people the attraction of mystical religions may be their emphasis on achieving a state of non-involvement with this world. If nothing matters, then nothing can cause you distress.

If a child is old enough for the opinion of her carers to matter and meets with a contemptuous response to the crying which signals her distress, she will feel a sense of shame. With constant repetition of the contempt, a person is created, who, whenever she has to cope with a difficult situation, immediately feels ashamed of her abilities and certain that she will fail at anything she attempts. She will be ashamed at school if she finds the work difficult or makes a mistake, and if the teacher is contemptuous or sarcastic the problem will be compounded sometimes to the extent of paralysing her capacities. The same reaction will dominate her work relationships. Underlying the shame, tears will always be waiting for an opportunity to burst through.

Some parents, with the same attitudes that tears are shameful, can, with the addition of lots of loving attention, use shame as a spur to the child to get approval from them and from the rest of the world. This is effective until the person is confronted by a distress which is more than temporary and before which she feels helpless, e.g. a long illness, unemployment or the death of a child. She is then having to deal with a deep and enduring distress for which she has only learned one response – shame and humiliation.

If, because of shame, we have suppressed our own tears and distress, we will avoid those of others, and if we are forced into a confrontation, contempt rather than sympathy is a likely response. The reality of someone else's suffering cannot be borne if one's own has never been accepted. If not treated with contempt it will be ignored, side-stepped, the conversation changed. The person complaining, friend, partner or child, will be forced to recognize that no comfort will be forthcoming.

Tomkins describes how making a child ashamed of tears can sometimes be combined with an emphasis on action to change or improve the situation which is causing distress. Here the impatient parent says something like, 'Now don't be a cry baby. Crying never solved anything. Stop crying and let's see what can be done. If you stop crying I'll help you'. In this way the child is made ashamed for two reasons. First she is ashamed just because she is crying. Second, she is ashamed because she is being passive and crying rather than being active and trying to do something about the problem.

This response emphasizes the problem rather than a recognition of the feelings of pain and distress associated with it. People who develop this attitude might well be attracted to law or welfare rights work, areas where circumstances can be dealt with and changed rather than feelings being acknowledged. Another person's problem produces an immediate offer of practical help but no response to the other's feeling.

There are certain people, well known to Citizens' Advice Bureaux and lawyers, who spend a lifetime in complaint, litigation and appeals for remedial action. They fill their lives by documenting the wrongs done to them by doctors, dentists, pension boards, social security offices. They exhaust the patience of even the most caring listener but no one, least of all the person himself, is aware that he is constantly on the point of weeping with distress. In his own mind he is perpetually coping with one minor crisis after another, but denies that these have anything to do with the inner life of feeling or with his personality.

Allowing a child, on a regular basis, to 'cry it out', alone and without comfort, is another way of inducing the shame/distress link. If the crying is intense and goes on for a long time until the child ultimately falls asleep or just gives up with exhaustion, the ultimate effect is often one of apathy and withdrawal of energy from the world. What is learnt by repetition of this experience is that to want something leads to pain and exhaustion.

There are adults who, when they have difficulty in solving problems, suddenly feel quite tired and exhausted – even to the point of falling asleep. The normal distress that anyone might feel becomes linked to earlier experiences of shame and weariness. This kind of link can also produce a profound resignation to destiny because of the feeling that when one most needs help, one's cry for help will not be heard, or if it is heard it will be ignored. Long, continuous experiences of crying to exhaustion will lead to pessimism as a fundamental approach to life. Such a person is always vulnerable. Someone who has not been allowed to cry in distress will spend much of his life seeking opportunities to cry in ways that do not bring punishment, e.g. in sad films, in the tears released when drunk or at funerals. On a Saturday night in a Glasgow pub, a mutual weeping session can be as satisfying as a fight. Some fantasies may be expressed in sado-masochistic behaviour where in mutual sexual excitement one can hurt and make one's partner cry while being hurt and crying oneself.

The capacity to trust the self and through that to trust others, is the only protection against what Becker describes as the ultimate human predicament, the realization of our human vulnerability, our existential loneliness. It is the basis of confidence and the capacity to be with other people in a cooperative and trusting way. By contrast the person who fails to achieve this is haunted all her life by a sense that she must meet trouble alone, must suffer in silence, can count on no one for sympathy or help and that if she were to surrender and cry for help, her tears would be met with contempt, hostility or rejection. This adult will seek no help from welfare services, will make minimum demands on her doctor, minister or priest, and under any circumstances will present a 'brave' face to the world and if necessary, die without complaining.

Some parents take the crying child, comfort it, but make no attempt to find the cause of the distress nor help the child to solve its problem. The child is given comfort but no solution. If this pattern is repeated, the individual as an adult will continue to look for sedation rather than solutions when she is lonely, baffled or sick and will find it in eating, alcohol, drugs, body contact with or without sex, warm baths or talking the hours away. These comforters can make people feel better on a short-term basis and, used wisely, can renew energy to return to the problem, but can become addictive alternatives.

Parents use a mixture of styles, depending on the mood they are in which can vary from one day to the next. Reactions to the child crying can also depend on what the parent reads into the cry. They may be sympathetic if the child appears to be in pain or has an accident but punish severely if the crying is caused by hurt following disobedience. The adult response is always related to the adult philosophy of suffering. It makes sense somewhere in the parent's mental map but an outsider, or their own child, may find the route taken a puzzling one. Children are remarkably skilled in picking up clues about the reactions they can expect from adults but for some children the complexities of adult reasoning defeat them utterly, and every encounter becomes a hazard. They live their later lives in a state of uncertainty.

Creative responses to distress

The most important positive response is not to allow the distress to become intensive or to last for any longer than can be helped. *Distress is a poison.* In very small quantities it can be biologically useful. Too much of it is dangerous. To pile fear and shame on top of the original cause distorts what can otherwise be a simple human experience. Most parents who cause an initial distress by, for example, shouting at the child or hitting them in a sudden discharge of hostility, regret it almost as it is happening. If they immediately comfort the child and apologize, no matter how young the child is, the incident can become a learning experience for both of them. Experiences of being helped and comforted enlarge the child's capacity to deal with their own distress. The experience of distress can offer an opportunity for the deepest intimacy and opportunities to express love and concern. This lesson is important for later behaviour with a partner in adult life.

A sympathetic parent can also direct the energy of some forms of distress into creative activity. Distress over school failure, if not followed by shame and recrimination, can lead to more concentration on work rather than on giving up hope and becoming disenchanted with one's capacity to succeed. Equally, helping a child to learn her French verbs or multiplication tables for the next test is as important as consoling her for failure in the previous one.

Consistent and creative help from parents in dealing with distress and its causes develops a sense of general trust in the parents and in human beings. This trust carries with it the conviction that when we are in trouble it will matter to someone else, that distress does not need to be a lonely experience and that sympathy and good feeling will be available. Distress can be seen as an occasion for intimacy and even as a situation which can be followed by joy. There is also an equally strong conviction that when we are too troubled to help ourselves, someone will both help us and best of all, help us to help ourselves.

A child can learn in the most positive way to feel sorry for herself and through that to feel genuine sympathy for other people. To be able to feel sympathy for oneself is a necessary prelude to being able to take action which will reduce the cause of the distress, rather than pushing the pain away, muffling it and not looking at it because we are ashamed of it. The stricture 'Stop feeling sorry for yourself' is as destructive as the linked phrase 'God helps those who helps themselves' when said to those convinced that not even God is interested in them.

Some stirring of sympathy for the self, rather than contempt for the self, may be the first step to self-respect. It is also the first essential of the capacity to help the self. Self-help groups are formed by people who care about themselves enough to try to improve their situation. One school of thought claims that sorrow for the self creates dependency, but this ignores the natural tendency of the human being to explore the world as soon as she feels safe. The capacity to feel sorry for oneself and to have that feeling respected is also a necessary basis on which to develop the ability to feel identification with other people who are suffering. Without that capacity it is impossible to create a sensitive and civilized world.

It is in the simple tasks of trying, failing, suffering, being comforted and trying again that the idea of progress is born and grows. Unrelieved suffering, either in childhood or in society, has never been the basis on which anyone has tried to build the New Jerusalem. We need to have encountered hope and sometimes to have had our hopes realized before we can conceive of changing the world for the better. It is not the totally oppressed who create revolutions. Demands come from those who begin to see the possibility of things getting better. It is through our experiences of distress and the way they are responded to that our vision of the world and what we can make of it is formed.

3

Boys, Men and Tears

BOYS DON'T CRY

'The boy is either very obstinate or very tough', he said to himself; 'in either case, another half dozen strokes won't hurt him, and he shall have them well laid on.' The new birch stung most cruelly, cutting crisp into the blistered wounds. It was as much as ever Charlie could do to keep quiet; and, struggle as he would, he could not restrain his tears.

Reverend Pullen, 1892, *Pueris Reverentia*.

What in the world is the use of a creature
All flabbily bent on avoiding the pitch
Who wanders about with a sob in each feature
Devising a headache, inventing a stitch?
There surely would be a quick end to my joy
If possessed of that monster - a feminine boy.

'The Female Boy', from *More Cricket Songs* by Norman Gale, 1905

The route to manhood is very hard for small boys. Like girls they start life locked into the warm sensual bliss of their mother's body, emotional and responsive. But by two years of age they are learning that they don't belong in that world. They have not to be like their mother, warm and receptive; they have to be like their father whose body is hard, not soft; who is energetic, not passive; and who is powerful, not weak. He learns that by having been born as a boy he is greatly privileged, so he must behave only like a man. If he behaves like a woman he will be punished.

Later in life, the theory goes, he will be allowed to go back to the softness of a woman's body; by then he will be strong and able to dominate her. If the conditioning has been successful, he will be able to take what he wants, not plead for it like a baby. If he fails to learn how to dominate a woman he will have failed to realize the most powerful myth of masculinity. Most families tell small boys quite clearly what is expected of them ... autonomy and aggression, in other words getting their own way and being prepared to fight for it. By eighteen months the patterns are already established. Girls have learned they are expected to be docile and sweet, hiding their aggression and anger because it's not tolerated.

But while the family influence is important, it needs the backing of society to reinforce its message and schools play an important part in driving it home. One book which looks at how this happens has the title *Boys don't Cry*, and the cover shows a small boy crying in bed. It gives an excellent description of ways in which masculinity is constructed but tears and crying are never once mentioned in the text. The nearest comment is that signs of 'vulnerability' are unacceptable in school. But the book does discuss some interesting questions. How do boys learn the kind of behaviour that tells the world that they are male creatures and not female? How do they learn to appear tough, independent, brave and unsentimental? In other words, how do those who may not have learned the lesson at home or in nursery school, now learn not to cry?

Having to attend school daily for three-quarters of the year from the age of five to at least sixteen is an important factor. In both single sex and mixed sex schools, assumptions and pressures combine to create a mental image of a man and how he is expected to behave; even more, how not to behave.

Clearly, social expectations of male behaviour start long before the age of five. One observer points out that if you took a baby out into the street and stopped the first twenty people you saw and asked them to hold 'Mark' and tell you what sort of baby he is, they would describe him as being bouncing, cheeky, mischievous and strong. Do the same thing with the same baby but call it 'Mary', and the responses will be that she is lovely, sweet, gorgeous, cute. By the age of eighteen months the child, boy or girl, has begun to have a sense of its gender, as a result of the behaviour of both parents and of other people in the environment.

Nursery schools reinforce this. One experiment showed that by two years of age both boys and girls were clear that girls would clean the house when they grew up and that boys would be boss and mow the lawn. This went hand in hand with behaviour from the adults who began to withdraw warmth and a show of open affection to the small boys as a way of encouraging 'manly' behaviour. By this stage some small boys are behaving in much more aggressive ways than the girls and while this causes much more trouble for staff, it is somehow partly accepted as how boys behave, although at this age biological factors are not thought to cause differences in behaviour between the boys and the girls.

Boys also seem to learn early that it is better, in the sense that life is more interesting and offers more choices, if you're a boy rather than a girl. This means that qualities associated with girls – passivity, gentleness, caring, the show of affection and feeling – are seen as inferior ways of behaving and must be avoided. After they start school, mothers are seldom allowed to kiss boys in public.

They are taught to value competitiveness rather than the collaboration which is so much more a feature of girls playing together; the intimacy which girls easily show to each other is derided and expressed where felt by a punch or a shove. Most of all, tears, which girls are usually allowed, are shameful. When, as inevitably happens with younger boys in a school, some failure or humiliation invokes tears in the classroom, the other boys freeze with embarrassment but later in the playground may persecute the weeper remorselessly. He has acted out their worst fears for themselves.

These young males develop the need to protect themselves from thoughts or information which might trigger off vulnerability. Many boys find it difficult to listen to each other. Almost before a sentence is finished they are challenging, deriding, contradicting. Listeners to Parliamentary broadcasts will recognize the phenomenon. Communication filters out 'feeling' material. They are in training for the male adult world of 'rationality' and 'objectivity' rather than the female world of intuition and sensitivity which is derided.

This means that the 'feminine' in themselves has also to be derided or denied and they learn to attack it in other boys. Some men have described how they used to bully other boys as a way of repressing their own tears. They might have left a painful emotional scene at home before coming into school, and rather than break down and weep they turned on some weaker boy and humiliated him. If he cried they got relief by jeering at him, and in that way regained control of their own feelings. With practice, they said, this got easier and painful feelings were replaced with cynicism or even hate for their parents who caused this pain. They learned to protect themselves by not showing vulnerability.

We know that bullying goes on in the army just as in schools. Any aspect of the young soldier that appears sensitive or vulnerable is a threat to the precariously-achieved masculinity of the others. Again, in bullying they are attacking what is most feared in themselves. The bullying, Rambo-style young man is in fact a liability to a modern army, which in occupied territories like those in Palestine or Ireland, has to win the minds and hearts of people and not just brutalize their bodies. The same applies to the young men going into the police force. The need of today's agents of social control is for sensitivity in the communities in which they are trying to keep order.

Both the Lockerbie disaster in Scotland and the Sheffield football disaster put young men into situations where their defences were swept away. At Lockerbie, young policemen and young soldiers had to scour the surrounding countryside carrying plastic bags into which they had to put the bits of legs, arms, heads and torsos of the crash victims. Going home at night in the buses, many of these young men wept. Even those who at first tried to use black humour as a defence were driven to silence. In the same way, the tragedy of the crushed bodies at the Hillsborough stadium caused young constables to weep with horror.

What is often forgotten is the strong military tradition which has never seen it as shameful to weep for the death of a comrade on the field of battle, as Achilles wept for his friend Patroclos outside the walls of Troy. The deaths at Hillsborough football ground, a place in many ways resembling a medieval battlefield, with its warriors on either side decorated in tribal colours, brought forth a display of young, male grief and weeping never before seen in public.

A modern version of hiding feeling is to be 'cool': in the sixties the phrase was 'laid back'. Essentially this is a protection against being hurt or showing vulnerability through ignorance. It takes the form of playing dead. This was in the past particularly an upper-class response, cultivated by the public school which was expected to train young men for posts in the empire and the army where they would face very complicated problems often with nothing but belief in their own natural superiority for support.

We no longer have an empire and the modern army asks for very different responses from its officers. An experiment has been going on in one of Britain's top public schools, Harrow, to break through this false mask which previous regimes had encouraged and to put the boys in touch with the reality of emotional life. Organized by the religious studies department as a way of making it respectable, the boys were brought together in small groups with girls from a neighbouring school to role-play a variety of human situations which embody powerful feelings. Some broke down in tears over situations like having to tell someone they had AIDS or when acting out the problems of divorced parents.

Attempts to teach about moral dilemmas in relationships and human development have been going on in state schools for many years but they tend to have low status. Many men teachers are unable to admit to vulnerable feelings and dismiss this kind of work as irrelevant for 'normal' boys. In one report the Department of Education and Science described a crucial aim of any form of education as the ability to understand oneself and act coherently. It would be good if that meant that boys need not hide their capacity to weep tears of sadness or tears of joy.

TEARS AND MEN

Men need to re-learn how to cry but first they need to unlearn their coping skills in emotional situations. I learned to hide, to pretend, to disguise my pain and hurt ... part banter, part clown, part indifference, part control, part aggression.

Man, in private letter.

The history of the emotional life of men is a neglected area of study. Everyone takes it for granted that men don't cry as much as women but few people question why that should be. One study on 'The inexpressive male', says quite simply, 'When a boy begins to express his emotions through crying his parents are quick to assert, "you're a big boy and big boys don't cry" '. Little boys are taught not to show emotions, especially tenderness and sadness. They learn that to be men they have to act rather than feel. Women, in most cases, are allowed to express love, happiness and sadness as part of their femininity. But for most men, to show feeling involves a loss of the sense of masculinity.

Just as women were trapped into roles of passivity and dependency, so men are trapped in roles of responsibility and strength. In times of severe hardship or danger, tears can't be tolerated lest they weaken determination to fight and struggle. To fight and struggle with full force demands that all tender feelings are abandoned. Energy has to go into winning. Only after the battle is over can you relax and then if you want to, weep with joy or sorrow.

Tears for the death of comrades have never been seen as demasculinizing. The Romans had tear bottles in which they collected their tears in order to demonstrate the extent and power of their grief. You may also, if you are very civilized, as was the Archbishop of Canterbury after the Falklands war, express sorrow not only for your comrades who have fallen, but also for your defeated enemy. The heroic tales of the Iliad are full of examples. Today we can see in the Olympics all the emotions nakedly expressed but we never see tears before a competitive event, only afterwards, in rejoicing or defeat. When men cry in ways that arouse sympathy, their tears are powerful. A television camera caught the vivid image of a boxer who had lost his fight bursting into tears. In a moment of insight the viewer could see this man's exhaustion and the melting of his ambitions. In the same way a young policeman seen weeping as he watched a video replay of his friend and colleague being killed was heartbreaking. We assume that the tears of men can only be justified by very powerful emotion – not the ordinary trauma of everyday life.

At the ending of the miners' strike in 1985, the *Guardian* newspaper's main headline read 'Pit strike ends in defiance and tears'. The article described how, a year after the strike had begun, the miners admitted defeat. Those waiting outside Congress House reacted with 'raw and unrestrained emotion'. When Arthur Scargill, after giving the news, went back into the building, one of the Scottish miners, at breaking-point, screamed at the walls of the building, 'We've given you our hearts, we've given you our blood, we've given you everything and then you sell us out. Davie Jones and Joe Green died on the picket lines for this and you turn round and slap us on the face . . .'. All breath and emotion expended, the miner collapsed in tears to be comforted by his colleagues. Several other miners wept at the decision. The following day the miners returned to work. I watched on television as they made a dramatic re-entry to the pits. At Mardy, in the Rhondda Valley, the colliery brass band played as 1000 miners and their families and friends walked through the traditional terraced streets with banners waving and heads held high. As they came up to the gates of the colliery the men linked arms. It was a moment of unbearable dignity and poignancy, and watching it I burst into tears. It was the sense of solidarity, of mutual caring and of having someone beside you in a heroic struggle that aroused such a powerful emotion.

If the miners' battle had been won there might also have been tears of triumph. These also fit men's image of themselves. These come often on the sports field after a titanic struggle and are shared by audience as well as players. They are particularly aroused by triumph which comes when the individual or the team has been on the brink of disaster – the runner coming from behind to win the race, the team that scores a try in the last minutes of the game that wins the match, the little man triumphing over odds. Yet these same men are often too embarrassed to say to their wives and children that they love them and need them.

Victorian men seem to have enjoyed more freedom to cry sentimentally than has been acceptable in the twentieth century. A famous singer, Tom Moore, could move his audience to tears during his drawing-room performances and men in the audience were said to creep out to sob noisily in the garden, one by one. Civil servants reporting to Parliament on the conditions of children working in the mines were known to weep. One famous parliamentarian, Sir William Harcourt after whom the stately Harcourt Room is named, was known to his contemporaries as 'Weeping Willie'. Winston Churchill, whose first twenty-five years were spent under Victoria, was always easily moved to tears. Harold Macmillan, an Edwardian, used tears as a craft when Prime Minister, seeing no shame in them. He seemed to have found them particularly helpful when negotiating with trade unionists. There are anecdotes of how, at appropriate moments, he always seemed able to summon up poignant memories of Paschendale and the brave young men who died there. He disarmed them by appealing to national pride.

By the second half of the twentieth century, tears were no longer acceptable in any aspirant for political leadership. They destroyed Edmund Muskie's career when he sought the American vice-presidential nomination. He wept in front of the cameras when asked an intrusive question about his wife, and from that moment his candidacy was doomed. On the other hand, Hawke, the Australian Prime Minister, during his election burst into tears when being attacked on television for a suspected involvement in drug-dealing. His reputation was in danger until it became known that his daughter was a drug addict. The tears worked in his favour because he became identified as a man whose tears could be turned to anger against drug pushers. The ideal politician is seen as strong, fierce in his protection of his country, able to be angry with enemies. Tenderness is not an asset.

In a steady progression from the nineteenth century, not only in Britain but in some European countries and in North America, manliness has become linked with control of feelings, courage, assertion and the capacity to endure without complaint. Darwin, who viewed tears as being rather lowly in the evolutionary scale, placed the Englishman at the peak of progress because he only wept 'under the pressure of the most poignant moral suffering', whereas, 'in certain parts of the Continent men would shed tears with great ease and abundance'.

In the industrial, competitive world, to succeed required free-dom from emotional dependence on other people – profit and sentiment don't mix. Feelings could 'threaten' a man's ability to think clearly and to act independently. In industrial society, man separated himself from the family leaving his wife to be responsi-ble for feelings of tenderness and vulnerability. Without independ-ence combined with hard work, self-advancement would not come, so the desired manly combination became autonomy com-bined with aggression, 'all in the service of intense competition for success in the market place'.

It can be particularly difficult to watch a man cry because of the message it carries of controls being broken down. When he stops he may feel humiliated at having been seen in that state. Women may find it particularly difficult to accept a man's tears if he is someone from whom she is seeking protection but who has consistently failed to provide it. Nora Ephron expresses this in her novel *Heartburn*:

> He looked at me – 'I'd like you to come back', he said. I shook my head, no, not because I was refusing but because I couldn't believe that that was all he had to say . . . Not a word about how he was sorry. Perhaps this is Mark's way of being understated, I thought . . . I kept shaking my head . . .
> 'I love you', he said. He said it with the animation of a tree sloth. 'I want you to come home. You belong at home . . . I know this is difficult for you', Mark said, 'but it's difficult for me too'.
> And then Mark started to cry. *Mark* started to cry. I couldn't believe it. It seemed to me that if anyone was entitled to cry in

this scene it was going to be me but the man had run off with my part.

Men say that women underestimate the burden of being a man and always having to accept responsibility for a dependent family. It must be terrifying to know you have to provide for your wife and children and perhaps an aging mother as well, not able to risk losing your job, yet not expected to show your fears. One man described having to hide his tears from his wife so as not to frighten her. He felt he had to treat her as a child rather than a partner. He is angry with the failure of the women's movement to acknowledge this burden and the trap into which men are born, locked into a masculine role. For some men this unfairness is symbolized by the fact that women can wear both trousers *and* skirts: they are allowed a freedom of role denied to men.

Except in extreme circumstances, tears in men are unacceptable in most of Europe, particularly in the northern Protestant areas and in North America. They must conceal all feelings of weakness, tenderness, dependency and sorrow. They must present themselves to other people as independent and tough. Tears become a symbol of weakness and femininity, something to be ashamed of and to be hidden. In the song, *Crying in the Rain*, the rejected lover says, 'If I wait for cloudy skies, you won't know the rain from tears in my eyes'.

One man told me how between the ages of eleven and twenty-eight he did not shed a tear. Even now, after years of trying to reverse this conditioning, he finds crying hard work. The independence he had so painfully achieved had been built on a denial of his need for love and comfort. This had resulted in his inability to tolerate any kind of dependency in others, particularly women friends. As a result as soon as they moved emotionally towards him, he was compelled to move away.

It is possible that sadness, particularly the sadness associated with loss and despair, can be identified from the earliest beginnings of life. Sadness may even be experienced before birth by the child in the womb, passed on by chemicals in the mother's blood. One man whose mother was a typist for the war tribunals in Germany after the Second World War, and who had to type terrible details about the concentration camps while she was pregnant, suffered throughout his life from depression. In analysis he made the connection and was able, by weeping, to let go of the sadness which he felt had been unwittingly shared with him.

Sadness is inherent in living, and by denying themselves the right to mourn, men deprive themselves of an important part of their humanity. They have forced themselves into a false heroism. Such a man was played by Clark Gable in the film *The Misfits*, written by Arthur Miller. Monroe plays the part of a woman who embodies women's vulnerability, and offers Gable an alternative view of a world where pain and feelings are not dismissed as irrelevant. The real confrontation comes when they set off in a group to capture wild horses, something he has done for many years, for them to be sold as riding ponies. But the world has changed; they are now used only as dog food and what had been a heroic activity is now a shoddy commercial undertaking. Seeing it through Monroe's eyes, after showing he can still master a wild stallion, he cuts it loose, mourning for the innocent world he has lost where he could be a hero.

Their 'innocent' world is lost but many men don't yet realize it. Americans who cling to the freedom to possess guns, which they see as symbols of frontier masculinity, don't seem to realize that this freedom leads to many squalid murders on the streets of their cities. The young soldiers on the streets of Belfast, Tel-Aviv or Beirut all harbour fantasies of masculinity and heroism that are irrelevant and outmoded. They are only acting out, at a local scale, the codes of the hawks of all nations who support a first-strike nuclear policy.

The world has changed: increasingly there are men who reject the masculine stereotype. They do not accept that there is some natural law which says men should never weep or cry nor be interested in children or cooking. These men feel they have been cheated out of important human experiences. They want to use their human capacities for tenderness and the ability to feel and to express love and sorrow. 'The more energy I use to control myself, the less able I am to be alive', said one of them.

Groups are coming together to make this possible. One, in Ireland, is the 'Men's Rather Loose Network'. At their first conference they talked about loneliness, a powerful aspect of sadness. They talked about their fear of showing feelings and the way in which much male behaviour which is described as chauvinist arises from loneliness and isolation, and the inability, which is so much a part of their tradition and conditioning, to communicate feeling. This affects their relationships with women, leading to rape, violence and promiscuity. Only by meeting together and talking with other men can these fears be faced.

I asked a number of men living in Scotland, who had been meeting regularly to discuss their conflicts about masculinity, about their tears. They said almost unanimously that they now cried about many different things but mostly when they were sad. Joy, anger, relief, even embarrassment, could also be triggers for tears but some had a set of inner scenarios to which they particularly responded. Reconciliations were high on this list, also children being abandoned, children being lost or frightened. They all found crying helpful in releasing tension. Some described how much more peaceful they felt afterwards but a few said that sometimes they felt their tears touched deeper feelings which were frightening. If they were to make contact with those powerful feelings they needed the company of someone with whom they felt safe and would know how to help them. Those who were not yet able to express themselves in tears felt afraid to let themselves go, but thought that with time their confidence would grow. They were just beginning to realize how strong the sanctions had been in their families against any show of 'weakness'.

Few could remember very early experiences of crying. Where they did it centred on being left alone either by their mothers or by whoever was caring for them. One painfully recalled how he had been tied up and ignored. Being a witness to parents arguing fiercely was a source of great distress which aroused fear and tears in young children. This crying often roused more anger in father who turned his wrath on them, so crying got mixed up with father's anger. For some their earliest memories were of being beaten by their father and shouted at for crying while the beating was going on.

One story was particularly poignant. For this man the word 'weeping' was inextricably associated with what he described as a famous and extremely haunting photograph from the Second World War. It is a picture of a middle-aged Frenchman, his face collapsed, tears streaming down his cheeks as he watches the victorious German army entering Paris. His own first memories of tears are associated with being savagely beaten whenever his father returned home from a sea voyage. After her death he realized that his mother had not bequeathed him a single act of kindness. She would present his father with a catalogue of the sins and misdemeanours the child had committed since his last visit home. His task on the first day of his return was to take the small boy to an unused bedroom and without saying a word, unbuckle his leather belt and ritually beat him with it. This man now weeps readily, but only for situations bound up with injustice. He believes these experiences in childhood explain to some extent the powerful impression made on him by the photograph of the middle-aged Frenchman watching the triumphant conqueror goose-stepping across his beloved country. I can't do better than use his own words. 'Across forty years two humiliations meet in recognition as they weep for the same thing and the same reason and the knowledge that the weeping will never cease.' I know of nothing which contrasts more powerfully with Rilke's description of love as 'two solitudes meeting to protect each other'.

Many of the men I talked with had been derided as children for crying, and spent years swallowing or hiding their tears. One, now a successful businessman, was one of the many victims of British imperialism. The only child of a civil servant stationed in the Far East, he was left at the age of four in a private children's home in this country. He remembered his mother leaving in a red car and then not seeing her for months. She did not say good-bye as 'that would only have encouraged emotion'. He trained himself not to cry and not to feel. By the age of six he finally managed to prove himself capable of resisting pain. Brought by his parents to a school in the Far East, he would allow the other boys to fire arrows made out of thorns into his bare legs. He would stand there in his short trousers and not make a sound. Looking down at the arrows sticking in his legs he knew that he had successfully vanquished feeling. He had made himself impenetrable and the other boys admired him for it. His impenetrability, his distance from his own feelings lasted for forty-four years, when he was at last able to cry as he told the story.

Even now most men could only cry with people for whom they felt deep trust but given a choice would prefer to cry with someone else than cry alone. One doctor felt he had made a very important step in being able to let his patients see his tears when they told him something very moving or if he was with them when a member of their family died. No one had gained enough confidence to be able to cry at a business meeting, but all had achieved the ability to cry at the theatre, the cinema or when watching television. In these situations they all recognized that it was a particular set of themes which triggered their tears. The most common was reconciliation but frequently themes which had their source in images of great beauty had a very powerful effect, such as a great eagle soaring in the high mountains. Some psychoanalysts believe that all tears are about existential loss, and that those who weep over beauty or freedom are weeping because they recognize its transitory nature.

There appear to be two-way links at work here: tears bring a release of tension – and a short spell of great mental clarity as the chatter in one's head dies down and the tautness of muscles is released – but release from other kinds of tensions as in reconciliations, at the end of a great musical performance, or immediately after the climax of a race or a rugby game can bring tears. Some men want to cry after a particularly satisfying sexual experience but they are afraid their partner may not understand.

Some gave themselves permission to cry, but others had only rediscovered that capacity to cry while in some form of healing relationship or formal therapy. Their reasons for going into therapy were usually difficulties with relationships. Finding the ability to cry and understanding the source of their tears became an important part of their healing. They rediscovered not only tears but other capacities for expressing feeling which had been buried with the tears. It wasn't easy.

For some men, falling in love in later life, with either a woman or another man, can have the same effect as going into therapy. This seems to be particularly so if the experience of love is doomed and fails. Tears come, perhaps for the first time for many years, for the loss of the loved person but they bring with them also tears for the lost life they might have had. It is as if they water the dried-up ground in which feelings have been suffocated and enable a late flowering. One man commented:

> As a man I find it hard work to find my tears. I often feel jealous of how easily women cry. Mostly my tears are hidden from me and I have to go looking for them. Intellectually I now know I need to cry just as I need to laugh and shout and yawn and fart.

When I asked these men what happened when they didn't cry it seemed clear that the feeling aroused didn't disappear. One man, if unable to cry, turned to compulsive eating. Others got headaches, constipation or pains in the neck. One man thought his feelings got turned in and added to what he called the 'garbage' he carries round with him until it all comes out in a great explosion of anger or rage. After this he is able to cry and express his sadness but always with regret for the damage he has done to his family while in a state of rage.

Some younger men talked about how they used anger as a way of avoiding tears, particularly in situations of humiliation. After being refused a job, one youngster described how he felt like bursting into tears but instead got himself out of the building and looking for release from tension took off his belt and began to lash out with the leather strap at the rows of cars he was passing. The anger intensified to feelings of revenge and he changed the end of the strap, using the buckle end to score deeply into the paintwork of the cars. He was ashamed afterwards but felt that what he had done was still 'better' than showing his feelings to a stranger.

This last response is a very important one. Work with groups of men who have been violent or batterers of their women partners and of children seems only to start being effective once the men have been able to express, with tears, the underlying sorrow they carry round with them. This unexpressed sorrow is converted into anger. The anger is blindly turned out against the world, often against women, not only because they are weak and therefore easy targets, but simply because they are there. The true source of their anger lies in the lack of comfort or protection they experienced from their own father, mother or carer. Frequently these men also find their own children intolerable if receiving the love and protection they were themselves denied. Their children become rivals for that scarce commodity, love.

Groups of men are meeting to work with topics like the beating up of women and children, rape and the sexual abuse of children. They invite men who have committed these acts to meet and work to change their behaviour. Their basic assumption is that all men – meaning all humans – are inherently good and innocent. If that is so, then something must have happened to account for all the bad things human beings do, including violence and child sexual abuse. What they claim happens is that we are hurt. If we lived in a perfect society, then we would deal with this hurt immediately by doing something like crying that would heal our hurts because it would identify and confront our pain. But if we are not able to discharge the hurts because of the prejudice against crying or the circumstances in which we live, then they hang around waiting for an opportunity to be dealt with. This means that every time we have to deal with a similar situation all the old feelings come rushing up again and we have to find some way of dealing with the suppressed pain. Violence against another is one response. Male violence, of course, is normally expressed against women and children. Women, would argue, and rightly, that we cannot excuse men's violence against women and children by recognizing that they too are hurt creatures. Women have been hurt as often as men but their response is not usually a violent one. Men's violence is linked-in to power relationships and these are taught and learned at every level of society. No matter how low down the social scale a man may be, there is always a woman or a child over whom he feels the right to exercise power. This has to be unlearned as the capacity to cry is learned.

One Glasgow man bitterly castigated himself for his behaviour towards his wife whom he is now learning not to use as a scapegoat. At first he said his tears after hitting her were only tears of self-pity, fear that she would leave him. He had no capacity to feel sorry for her, only for himself. Now, he says, he is getting closer to his own pain and believes this is giving him the capacity to cry for her as well as for himself. For the first time he is trying to see her not just as *his wife*, but as a human being with her own life and needs.

An American men's support group believes that the taboo men carry against showing feelings has very negative effects on many aspects of their lives. Their fear of losing control and therefore of losing power dominates much of their behaviour. They are reluctant to ask for help, even to the extent of stopping and asking for directions at a petrol station if they are lost: how much less are they able to ask for help or even information about their sexuality, their relationships with parents, lovers or friends. When they most need help they are most likely to isolate themselves.

Men who are released from their masculine roles by virtue of bisexual vocations like writing, acting, dancing or painting – the creative arts – may be more able to cry than those in more rigid or conventional occupations. Scott Fitzgerald used to cry over his own stories and on one occasion recalled how 'riding in a taxi one afternoon, between very tall buildings and under a mauve and rosy sky, I began to bawl because I had everything I wanted and knew I would never be so happy again'. He had also great sensitivity about situations which involved another's tears. Writing about his wife Zelda, he described poignantly how on a journey with him which was filling her with nostalgia, she suddenly began to cry.

'Zelda was crying, crying because things were the same and yet were not the same. It was for her faithlessness that she wept and for the faithlessness of time'.

It may be that such men are simply released to use what for convenience we call the 'female' part of themselves, just as a more equal society would allow women to use their masculine characteristics. Jung held that each of us has an *animus*, the male principle, in our personalities and also an *anima* or female principle. This was a way of describing that range of characteristics that have become associated with each sex – hardness versus softness, strength versus gentleness. In societies where life is very harsh we tend to find that the differences between men and women are most clearly polarized, while in more affluent societies it becomes possible for men and women to share a wide range of capacities.

No emotions are 'wrong'. Everything depends on the context in which they are used. Sometimes anger, fear, weeping are useful for either men or women: sometimes they may be inappropriate. What is important is that they should be available to us if we want to use them.

In his book about the American rock music industry, *Sweetie Baby Cookie Honey*, Freddie Gershom describes how his hero was able to rediscover his capacity to feel in grieving for the death of a close friend:

His body shook violently and, like a dam bursting, the tears began to flow, slowly at first, then uncontrollably. His chest heaved with racking sobs – he could barely keep his balance. His nails dug into his palms. He cried out in burst of agony and leaned his head against the coffin edge.

For once he didn't care what he looked like. He didn't think, he didn't hold back, he wasn't performing or pretending. At last, there was no audience to perform for. If he hadn't cried for Rick, he would never have cried. If he hadn't felt now, then his feelings would surely be dead and he wouldn't deserve to be alive.

The tears flowed and his body grew weak and the hysteria subsided. When he finally caught his breath, his body tingled with a strange new feeling of release. Somehow, the barrier that had surrounded him for a lifetime seemed weakened. He could feel it inside and out. This was the cry he'd been suppressing for a lifetime, the cry of feeling, passion, and emotion that, bottled up inside him, had been aching for release. He felt the pain of Rick's death like a needle through his heart – but *he felt*, and that was Rick's most profound bequest.

There is a long history of men weeping for the loss of their close friends, but men need not just a few moments of release, but a lifetime. The homosexual movement should be thanked for its claim that men should have the freedom to express their feelings as freely as has been allowed to women. Sadly the AIDS virus has given a generation of young men, who otherwise would not have had to confront their own mortality for many years, experiences of their vulnerability. The loss of their partners and lovers has obliged them to experience and endure a wider and deeper range of feelings than they were originally asking for in wanting to express openly their love for other men. Now they are also claiming their right to show their grief. Some of the most profoundly moving and creative ideas about the human condition are being expressed by these young men, not only those who have lost their loved ones, but those who are currently facing the disintregration of their own bodies, the loss of their own lives.

4
Women and Tears

Surely, surely, they should both ... be embracing each other and comforting each other and weeping. But human beings are endlessly ingenious about promoting their own misery. Even in catastrophe mysterious barriers can isolate them, barriers of fear and suspicion and sheer stupid moral incompetence.

Iris Murdoch

Even the most loving woman is sometimes angry and feels passionately that there are things she lacks which she is entitled to have. Many have been taught that in a relationship they have no right to make demands on a partner; to say clearly what they want may lose his affection. It can be even more complicated. A woman may feel that if she expressed herself honestly, she would not only lose her partner's affection but her self-respect by being selfish and unfeminine.

So often her only resource is tears, and those tears will more likely arouse panic rather than understanding from the man with whom she is trying to communicate. For her the tears are a language, for him they are a threat. Woman after woman has told me how their partners couldn't bear them to cry. 'If I cry, he just walks out', said one. 'If I cry, he gets so angry that I can't bear it', said another, 'and I go away and find somewhere by myself where I can go on crying'. 'But it's a terrible feeling', said another, 'not to be able to cry with the most important person in your life. The tears aren't the same somehow if you've got to cry alone. They don't heal you in the same way if you can't share them'.

These women saw their tears as an important source of release from tension, yet they had been unable to persuade husbands or partners to be comfortable when they were crying, just to be there and let them cry. 'He always wants to do something to stop me crying', was a frequent comment. 'If I'm crying because someone's been nasty to me, he'll want to rush away and knock their block off', said one woman, 'for anything else he'll just sit there and look miserable and uncomfortable until I feel I'm supposed to comfort him'.

It became clear talking with women that many men find it difficult to offer comfort. They seem unskilled in the simple acts that console women when they are distressed – like being held gently for as long as they need to be held, making murmuring noises rather than using words (or even worse, forming sentences), wiping tears away and blowing noses ... in other words giving the same comfort which you would give to a child. The experience, from what women say, is most helpful when it is non-verbal. Sounds are all right but words, particularly logical words, tend to activate those parts of the brain that include judgemental and evaluative awareness of the self. For some of the initial stages of crying, the length of time needed simply to weep, varies from person to person, it seems that the important thing is an unhurried, quiet, non-judgemental and shared experience.

Most women offer this to each other when they cry together. To watch women comfort each other can be a deeply moving experience which rolls back centuries of shared experience of the burden of living. Such precise understanding of their needs, expressed by many women, may be related to earlier good experiences of being comforted by their own mothers. But presumably men were comforted in the same way, so why are they, unlike women, unable to pass it on?

For some men, the tears of women with whom they are closely involved may arouse anxiety, provoking memories of their mother crying. This may reactivate feelings of helplessness and fear because the person to whom they look for comfort is herself vulnerable. Some unhappy women, whose husbands are unable to offer them emotional support, quite inappropriately turn to their sons. The conflict aroused in these male children can induce an emotional paralysis in later life.

But equally, the buried incestuous temptation invoked by the seductive mother may result in the same man being profoundly moved and sexually attracted to distressed women for whom he has no emotional responsibility. Few things are more infuriating for a woman who is denied comfort for her own tears than to see her partner being sympathetically and sensually attracted to a strange woman who is grieving. This is often what lies behind the suspicion which is aroused by widows, divorceés, and unhappily-married women whom men who already have partners are so keen to help. What the widow, divorceé or sorrowing woman fails to realize is that if the grieving were to stop the interest might diminish, or if intimacy were to develop to the point of involving responsibility, comfort would be withdrawn.

It may be that the defences against their own feelings which they learned makes it impossible for men to tolerate the intense show of feeling from their women partners which is implicit in weeping. If you are not allowed that kind of release for yourself, it may be intolerable for you to see someone else using it. There is an additional double bind for men in that they are very often the cause of the woman's tears; it may well be their behaviour that has caused the distress. How do you comfort the person to whom you have done an injury, particularly if you reject the idea that your behaviour carried any cause for reproach?

Men are taught from their earliest days to value autonomy, the right to do what they want to do, when they want to do it. Women, because of the nurturing and caring roles allocated to them, the responsibility they are given for the well-being and happiness of children and of men, are much more likely to be taught the value of submitting to one's fate and considering the needs of others before their own.

I have stated those two positions very crudely: in fact both are extremely complex and each represents a sophisticated view of the world. They can be described in many other ways, as yang and yin, as materialism and spirituality, as individualism and cooperation. They can be blended, but too often in our secular society, they are poorly-understood styles of behaviour acted out between men and women in conflicting ways. Tears from the woman, which with more understanding could create a bridge between the two positions, more often intensify the barriers.

There are, of course, many men who have the capacity to offer comfort and who are at ease with their partner's tears. We know little about them, presumably because their partners do not complain. It is fair to speculate a little about what kind of men these may be. They are probably at ease not only with women's tears but with a range of private feelings and needs for dependency and intimacy. They have enough inner strength not to feel threatened by the demand for child-like dependency implicit in tears; they will recognize it for what it is, a temporary rather than a permanent threat to their autonomy. They will not automatically feel manipulated. Most importantly, the event will be experienced by them as a reality which is happening in the here and now and not as a replay of frightening and damaging early experiences. They will 'see' the woman who is crying as herself and not as some emotional ghost from the past. They will probably be able to respect their own tears and if they have children they will be able to respect their tears. One young woman who talks lovingly about her tears, told me how her father used to say, 'It's Fred inside you watering the iris in his window boxes'.

Many women described the particular pain of not being able to share their tears. They spoke of the loneliness and sense of abandonment, and the way in which this interfered with the use of tears as a healing experience. Crying alone, when their partner was actually in the same house but chose not to be with them, was an exhausting and draining experience. They emerged dry-eyed but also with a dry heart. After a succession of these experiences their capacity to cry at all may even dry up, along with the relationship between themselves and their partner. The comparison with the experience of children left to cry alone without being comforted is obvious.

For women who share a home, finding some place to cry is not always easy, particularly if there are children whom you are protecting from your distress. The bedroom can be a retreat but it can also be a bitter reminder of the comfort you would like to be getting from your partner. Lying weeping alone on a double bed can impregnate the room with associations which will leave doubts about the validity of the tenderness which is offered along with sexual encounters. Weeping in the lavatory or bathroom is hazardous because of the chance of interruptions and many women find the setting vaguely demeaning. 'If I want to cry, I hide in the toilet and feel desperate', was a common reaction if I asked someone where she cried. It can also revive memories of childhood tantrums and distress, locking one's self in the lavatory or bathroom and shutting out the adults who came battering at the door. Children who do this are making a statement about not needing comfort from adults, while at another level needing them desperately and choosing a place where they know they will be forced out.

Some women feel themselves driven out of the house, unable to tolerate sharing space with a partner so palpably ill-at-ease with her tears. One told me how on a cold winter's day of driving rain, her only refuge was the car parked outside the house. She was too shaken with sobs to risk driving so she sat there for two hours weeping her heart out while neighbours and passers-by studiously ignored her obvious distress. Women with more mechanical confidence will drive off, going sometimes for miles with tears pouring down their face, until they find a quiet lay-by to work through the final stages of their process.

Others with no cars walk through the streets or find a near-by park. The more fortunate may have a close friend who can offer the comfort unavailable at home. Some may even go back to mother for comfort, but that can be a double-edged solution. The complex relationship between mothers and daughters may arouse feelings of dependency and failure which further confuse the issue that sparked off the tears.

One of the hardest things for women to bear is the way men reject tears as silly and irrelevant, when they know them to be important and valuable. The most powerful function served is the release of tension. The tension comes from many sources: anger, fear, shame, helplessness, sorrow, repentance.

Why do I cry? I cry to release huge waves of feelings which can build up, especially when I cannot or dare not put feelings into words. The dare-not feelings are usually anger. I fear it will go out of control so I release it in tears either by myself or with someone I love and trust. If I'm angry with someone I love and trust, I can express my anger in tears with them; if I am angry with someone I do not love, then I withhold my tears – to be expressed later, in a safe situation, or not at all. If I hold back the tears, the feeling becomes locked or blocked in my body.

A musician adds to the story.

Anger tears are my Beethoven tears, wild and crashing. Other tears flow more from the solar plexus – my tear fountain – they are my Strauss tears, or more recently Berlioz's *Nuits d' Ete*, certain pieces by Chopin, Elgar Cello concerto, Brahms violin concerto, the slow movement in Schubert's string quartet, some of Bach's choral music . . . the list goes on. These pieces speak to me of boundless beauty and passion and I rejoice in my tears – but I use them too, intuitively, when I feel depressed or despairing, to release tears. Music, tears, song, breath are so closely linked for me – like a great life giving force.

I can't stress too much the value I give my tears . . . they are priceless, beyond words, they are the most private part of myself that I can share with those who draw close to me. They give me life and hope, they renew me.

These are women holding on to the value of their tears, but there are many others who have been made to feel ashamed.

It is such a secret place, the land of tears.

Antoine de Saint Exupery

The most frequent messages given to women are that tears are a sign of weakness, or instruments of manipulation. One young woman who uses tears very creatively in her life and also in her work as an actress asserted very positively:

I don't think that crying is a sign of weakness as it's so often made out to be. I feel very strong when I cry. It's a sweet strength like my body's poetry. It's at the edge of things.

Tears are clearly woven through her life in a natural way.

Sometimes I go without crying for some while and then I go through phases of crying rather a lot. Of course tiredness affects it as do my periods and the time of the day even. Sometimes my tears are so hot they feel as if they've been baking inside me, sometimes they feel bigger and wetter, sometimes rather lighter and not so salty. Sometimes I have to make a lot of noise with them and move my body with them like passion – and sometimes they just slide out very gently and don't affect me so much, like a cooling system.

In this extraordinarily intuitive and perceptive account of her relationship with her tears this young woman has confirmed many of the research findings of scientists interested in the physiology of tears. She sees her tears as meeting a variety of her needs. She recognizes how they interact with her body chemistry, tiredness or her period. Even the time of day is relevant. Different kinds of need alter the quality and the quantity of the flow. She uses her tears as a natural antidote to tension and stress, which is one of their most important functions.

Women who get relief and even enjoyment from crying can

share this knowledge, given even modest encouragement. One day, in a Glasgow clothes shop, the assistant, an attractive and helpful young woman, asked what kind of work I did. I explained that I was trying to understand the part tears play in our lives. Her face lit up. 'Oh, I love my tears', she said. 'I cry all the time, when I'm happy, when I'm sad, when I'm making love. It's terribly important to me'. She told of the one time when the weeping stopped. When she was about twenty, she worked in an office, one of two women among about thirty men. Late one afternoon, after a particularly demanding day, she sat down at her desk and burst into tears. The other woman, whom she described as a man-hater, made her get up and come to the lavatories and once inside shouted vehemently, 'Don't you ever do that again, if those men see you crying they'll walk all over you'. The shock was such that she stopped crying immediately, but what was worse, she stopped crying at home as well and felt simply awful, physically and mentally, until able to cry again.

I asked her if her husband minded her tears. 'He's used to it now', she said. 'At first he was frightened. Especially when I wept after we'd made love. He'd ask if he'd hurt me, but now he's used to me', and she laughed with pleasure.

COUPLES

When a woman weeps she weaves snares.

Cato

Women recognize that some of their tears are tears of weakness, and these are the tears which come as an alternative to rage and anger or as a way of coping with their feelings of powerlessness. Most women find it very difficult to express anger openly and honestly, particularly to men. They also find it hard to cope with men who are angry with them. Women learn at an early age that most men do not like angry women living in the same house. In abstract they may admire and be excited by them, but their day-to-day preference is for women who want to please them and don't make too much of a fuss. Modern men also stipulate that they mustn't be boring, without seeing any contradiction in that thought.

Girl children learn these messages in subtle ways. The most obvious is by watching father's reaction to mother's behaviour and the comments of both about other women and other marriages. But the most powerful is the father's reaction to his daughter's femininity and the part she has to play as 'Daddy's little girl'. The more charming, cuddly, loving and even manipulative she is, the more rewarded. 'She can twist me round her little finger', is said with glowing pride. Very few fathers would actually prefer to have a strong-minded, independent daughter who put her own needs before his and was able to criticize his behaviour openly. Since father's approval is such an important factor in the life of most women they will develop skills to avoid losing that approval. If the show of anger is unacceptable it is repressed. But feeling does not evaporate: if it cannot be shown in one form it finds an outlet in another. This is where that marvellous rag-bag of feeling we relieve through our tears comes to our aid. Tears can be another face of anger, a form of relief for the intolerable tension and frustration of not being able to show what we are thinking and feeling.

The women who talked to me about using their tears to deal with anger, recognized quite clearly what they were doing. Most either thought it didn't matter as long as they got relief for their tension and frustration and saw it as a way of keeping the peace, but some were trying through women's groups or assertion therapy to express themselves more honestly. They had become aware of their fear of sharing feelings with their partners and saw this as an unhealthy way to live. They were mostly younger women.

But there was a very small group who acknowledged that their unspoken anger was so powerful, they used their tears as a revenge, knowing that their husbands hated tears and knowing that weeping they could discomfort them. Their marriages had fallen on stony ground but it seemed to me there was still hope. As long as the tears are coming, energy can be redirected.

The balance of power

For tears have run the colours from my life.

Wordsworth

The powerlessness of women is seldom understood except by

those experiencing it. 'Robert didn't say I must go back to work after the baby', Lucy told me, 'but he began to be reluctant about switching on electric fires and looking disapproving if I did'.

He took over total control of the finances and the cheque book. I had to account for every penny I spent, but he never told me what he was spending. He started leaving a ten pound note on the table every morning when he went out to work. Some mornings he would rush away and forget to leave anything. If I noticed in time I would have to run after him and ask for it. I would come back into the house feeling so humiliated that I would just sit down and cry and then the baby would start crying so I had to stop.

For the first time in our marriage I began to tell him lies. I had a little money saved and I began to use it up. When I bought something I'd say it was less than it really was. I wouldn't tell him if I went for lunch with my mother or a girl friend and I paid. I couldn't bear that they should always pay for me because I didn't want them to know how awful Robert had become. Then my money ran out and I stopped going out at all. I got more and more depressed. Sex was awful. If I didn't want it he would say that he was keeping me and the least I could do was give him sex. So after that I just lay there and let him do what he wanted and he would complain about that too. He would go to sleep and I would lie there with tears running down my face thinking how good it had been before the baby came. If I tried to talk to him, I used to start crying and he would say, 'Oh God!' and tell me I was useless.

With the help of a friend Lucy stopped crying and started being angry. She found a childminder and went back to work. She doesn't cry in front of Robert any more, she still tells him lies about what things cost so that she can save some money and make sure she'll never be dependent on him again. She has also decided not to have a second baby.

Lying in bed, after sex, silently weeping when your partner has gone off to sleep, is an experience many women are familiar with. The sexual life of the young exhausted mother of a fractious baby takes on a dream-like quality.

'I'm too tired even to object', said one drained looking young woman. 'He just keeps telling me that he loves me and needs me.

All I can think of is not wakening the baby, so I say OK and he goes ahead. One night I was so tired that I fell asleep when he was still pushing in and out of me. I wakened up when he started shouting at me. Then he turned away and went to sleep and I lay there and wept, feeling an absolute failure'.

For women trying to survive in the game of life there are few ways of improving the balance of power within the family (or within the workplace). The main one is to put pressure on relationships to create anxiety or guilt or the urge to care for and protect the 'weaker' partner. She may need money to buy food for the family, or she may be trying to stop him leaving her and the children. There is a long list in between.

A woman can present herself in various roles: as a 'mother figure', or as a child appealing to her husband's paternal instinct. The mother image can be either the strict mother who has to be obeyed, or else the loving mother who has been hurt and can now be comforted. The strict mother can be very effective in getting what she needs if the man's early experience helps him to relate to that kind of woman. Her style is to bully, not to weep. But behind the bullying often lie tears. Behind the loving mother who appeals through tears will lie anger. Depending on her partner's previous life experience, anxiety or guilt or caring can be aroused. A few preliminary skirmishes in the early stages of the relationship will make it clear how the man is going to react to tears. If, as sometimes happens, anger is aroused, the woman's claim is lost and she should save her tears. Richmal Crompton offered one possibility in the William stories.

> Violet Elizabeth dried her tears. She saw that they were useless and she did not believe in wasting her effects. 'All right', she said calmly, 'I'll thcream then. I'll thcream, and thcream, an thcream 'till I'm thick'.

For those unable to be so direct, the bed can become, for the angry woman, an arena of struggle, perhaps the only one in which she has the advantage. She can if she chooses convert the pain, the humiliations, the tears of every other situation in which she is disadvantaged, into revenge, contempt and victory. Unless the husband is a violent man, the wife can dictate how often sex will take place. The cynicism which grows out of not having her tender feelings acknowledged and valued replaces the openness and tenderness with which she first entered into the partnership.

> Twice a month's about right for me. That satisfies my sexual need which is actually stronger than some of my friends, and it's often enough to take the edge off him. What I don't want is to do it so seldom that he gets angry; because he does if he has to wait too long. Also I don't want him to try to have it off with someone else. I've cried enough trying to get him to understand that there's a difference between a good fuck and a good shit.

Most partnerships involve tentative negotiations until they find ways of communicating that suit each of their needs. Mostly these are the best that can be managed in what is basically an inequitable relationship. Tears become a signal to the male partner that the issue under discussion is one that should be taken seriously, and if he is sensitive to his partner's needs he will respond swiftly and allow the woman to weep in ways that affirm her dignity. One husband described to me how he has learned to interpret the various kinds of tears his wife sheds.

> When she's crying with pain for something like a migraine headache, I just sit in the dark with her and hold her hand. If she's crying for some other reason like because we've been quarrelling and she wants to make up but doesn't know how to I just put my arms round her and cuddle her and let her cry it out. Until she's done that I know I won't get any sense out of her. I try to work out if she's got a period due or if she's been having trouble with her mother. If we've been quarrelling, after she's stopped crying I really try to understand what she was on about. It must mean a lot to her if it made her cry.

That's a very different response from the man whose anxiety or guilt are aroused by his partner's tears and shouts, walks away or who gives in to a woman's demand without trying to understand what's 'going on'. Handling it in this way is likely to leave him with a sense of confusion and resentment. She in turn may hope that in time she will get the caring response she is really seeking and will pursue the pattern. This tragic game can go on for the rest of their lives or one of them can decide enough is enough and withdraw.

Conscious manipulation of tears is very rare, although most women acknowledged how powerful tears can be and could

remember the odd occasion on which they had been used as a
weapon when all else failed. Manipulative tears were seldom used
with someone close. It was more likely to be someone for whom
they had no personal feeling. One young woman claimed to have
wept her way into a degree but once started on work and a career,
never used such tricks again. What she said she did with her tutors
at crisis times was not deliberately engineer tears, which is quite a
difficult thing to do, but not hold them back.

Women who told me that their partners accused them of using
tears to manipulate them agreed that there were times when they
deliberately wept, but said that it was often the only way they
could get their partner's attention. Even then they didn't actively
manufacture the tears. They were always lying just below the
surface of their life. Often the choice was to weep or else to hit their
partner over the head with an axe or say really horrible things to
them. In fact many women said it was kinder to cry than to be
angry because, they claimed, if they said what they were really
thinking their husbands would be so incredulous and so humiliated that the marriage would not survive.

One woman had looked up the meaning of manipulate in the
Oxford English Dictionary. It meant, she discovered 'To handle,
especially with dexterity'. Only in the nineteenth century did it
begin to include the *unfair* management of people or things. 'Well',
she said, 'I have *had* to manage my husband. If I hadn't we'd never
have survived and we certainly wouldn't have the standard of
living we have now. I should be congratulated not criticized, and if
sometimes I've been a bit unfair, played a bit of a game, that's life
isn't it. If he'd been stronger I wouldn't have needed to because
then he'd have looked after me'.

Time and time again discussions about tears came back to the
central theme of the wish to be cared for – not all the time, the
women with whom I talked were quite clear about that. But what
they all wanted was to be cared for *some* of the time and often their
tears were statements about that need. The need did not seem to
me, in most cases, to be neurotic in the sense of being unhealthy. It
was rather a simple and healthy statement of a basic right in a
partnership to be nourished by one's partner.

Women at work have a triple difficulty to cope with. They have
fewer opportunities than men to be nourished by their work, since
they are more often involved in dull and repetitive jobs; secondly,
the domestic and nurturing skills in which they have usually been

trained are held in lower esteem both in the home and in the workplace than administrative or management skills, so what they do is less likely to receive praise; lastly, they are conditioned to value praise from men more highly than praise from women, who are more often their colleagues or first-level bosses. In an organization, they may rarely come to the attention of a predominantly male management in ways that give them power and encouragement.

These facts make them more reliant than they should be on the good opinion of their partners. They want to be praised for skills which their partners may see as trivial, like cooking, creating a welcoming and attractive home and the care of children. If what they do day in and day out is ignored or not valued, they feel not valued. Depression, which is expressed in tears, can follow or else a sense of outrage at not being taken seriously, which can explode in the form of tears of rage. A partner may not detect the difference and the woman herself may be confused.

Feminists argue that women should not be so dependent on the opinion of men. A woman's sense of validity should lie in her feelings about herself. While this may be true, we should remember the fragility and plasticity of the human psyche. Even if someone becomes self-confident and inner-directed, that has to be constantly reinforced in the wider society if those attitudes are to be maintained. A year at home with a small child and no recognition by a partner of the importance and difficulty of that role can reduce the most competent career woman to an anxious or depressed wreck.

It's not only a problem between women and men, though that is where it is most frequently seen. Exactly the same problems can emerge in gay and lesbian partnerships where there is inequality of power and opportunity. It is true that women in the main tend to be more lovingly affirming of each other, and use less competitive and down-putting styles of relating than men, but the problem is not only personal: it is embedded in all our social structures.

The new and more powerful roles offered to women in the world of work may diminish their powerlessness before men and change the way working couples relate. But this change is needed also with couples where the woman caring for children is placed in a dependent role. Women have to claim their right to be angry, but men have to claim their right to weep and show fear if the balance is to change. What we need is for all of us, men, women and children, to be open to and comfortable with all these feelings.

There are times when the way a woman uses her tears in a relationship is a barrier to her growth. She may not have had any opportunity to understand their capacity to nourish her emotional life. One woman had used tears and tantrums to get her own way in every conflict with her husband. This was how she had coped with a desperate childhood of loss. These were the only weapons she had had against an apparently uncaring world, and through using them she retained a precarious sense of identity and integrity. When she married she continued to use these techniques although they were no longer relevant in a relationship which required different skills, but for her, this was a foreign country. The marriage ended when her husband gave up the struggle to find better ways of communicating with her. She continued her angry and frustrated weeping, but was forced to question herself when her son also withdrew and gave his support to his father. At this point she showed enormous courage by re-assessing her life, and has now struggled through to what she describes as a liberating philosophy of autonomy and self-determination. She no longer reacts blindly to every conflict. She is modest, feeling she has taken only the first steps. For her at this stage, not crying is a great achievement but she hopes that some day she will reach a better balance so that her tears will be for herself rather than to make an impression on others.

LOVE, LOSS AND TEARS

'(Wo)man is not destroyed by suffering. (S)he is destroyed by suffering without meaning'

What Camus might have said.

For most women, the most powerful source of their tears lies in their relationship with men, and particularly their experiences of being abandoned. To lose love through death is hard but understandable; to lose love and not understand why is intolerable. For many this situation induces a kind of frenzy. They may weep until they can weep no more, they may rage, they may scream, they may become ill. What they want more than anything else is to understand why this has happened to them. And some of them will go to extraordinary lengths to try to find out.

If a woman's relationship with a man breaks down, and he abandons her, she will usually blame herself, having been taught that success in personal relationships is her responsibility. If she has lost her partner to another woman, it will be assumed that she must be more beautiful, more clever, more sexy: in fact she wants her to be. That would make sense.

A stunning young woman whose husband left her for a woman twenty years older than himself, never forgave him for it. He had questioned a fundamental tenet of her life, that young women are more attractive than older women. Her self-confidence never recovered, since if her belief was right there must have been something else wrong with her, some terrible ugliness from which he had fled even into the arms of an older woman.

Where the other woman is not known fantasy can run riot. The other becomes a witch, an evil enchantress, with amazing powers to seduce the innocent. Efforts are made to find out more about her, sometimes with extraordinary ingenuity. The energy put into this can be manic in quality, a white heat of power that other women will understand but most men find frightening.

Ann's lover simply stopped coming to see her, giving her no explanation. The relationship on his side had clearly been casual, never serious or even regular, but she became very emotionally involved and hoped it would develop. She tried phoning him with a variety of invitations she felt he wouldn't refuse, but he always made excuses for not meeting her. Knowing something of his work and leisure patterns, she tried meeting him 'accidentally' coming out of his office or at his local pub, all to no avail. She became convinced that he had found another woman and concentrated on trying to find out who she was. She sent him theatre tickets for two anonymously and bought herself one for a few seats further back. Two strangers used the seats. She took to following him in her car, being willing to sit for hours outside his house waiting for him to come out and then trailing and following him until he came home again. All her energy was focussed on his life and what he was doing. Her own life and work faded into insignificance. One night, waiting in her car outside a pub to which she had followed him, she suddenly found herself crying for the first time. She says she wept nonstop for an hour during which she gradually began to realize that she had been out of her mind for the last six weeks. As she wept she allowed the pain of the loss of her man to become real. She went home and the next morning began rebuilding her life.

Jane had been sharing her life and home with a partner, John, for four years. His firm sent him for a month to another part of the country, and at first he telephoned home every night; but three weeks later she got a letter saying that he had met another woman and was planning to marry her as soon as possible. She can't remember how she spent that day but has a vague memory of being like a wild animal howling through the house, tears pouring down her face, drinking brandy, tearing at her clothes, pulling his clothes out of the wardrobe and holding them close to her, burying her face in them, trying to recover the smell of him. The prophet Micah's image of desolation is very similar: 'Therefore I will wail and howl, I will go stripped and naked: I will make a wailing like the dragons, and mourning as the owls'. Terrified to telephone and hear him say the words he had written on paper, she collapsed ultimately into a drunken stupor – a woman who had never previously drunk more than a half bottle of wine.

For several days she stayed off work and continued to weep helplessly until exhausted. Her head gradually began to clear. She resolved to find out about the other woman. She had almost lost interest in the man but felt obsessed with the woman who had made such an impression in such a short time. Her partner's passionate hobby was shooting, and she knew from their telephone calls that he had been spending his spare time at a sports club which had a range. Her brain was more active than ever before. She hunted down the telephone number through directory enquiries and then rang. She asked for the secretary and launched on a long story about phoning from a restaurant where a pair of leather gloves had been found apparently left by the lady with Mr Johnston whom one of the waiters had remembered seeing at the sports club. Would the secretary know if Mr Johnston had a wife who might have been with him?

The secretary laughed and said he thought he could guess who that was. No it wasn't Mr Johnston's wife, he didn't have one. His guess was that they belonged to another of their members. Should he pass a message on? 'No', said Jane, 'but if you could give me her telephone number I'll ring and arrange to have them delivered'. 'No trouble', was the response, and the number was found. Jane could hardly believe it had been so easy. The next step was to 'phone. When a woman's voice answered she had to hang up, her anger was so powerful. She sat down to recover, but it was an hour before she could dial again.

This time she was prepared and she launched quickly into a story that she was a freelance journalist doing an article for the women's page of a national newspaper about women who joined sports clubs. Could she do a telephone interview? It worked and for the next half hour she was able to quiz the woman whom she saw as having stolen her happiness on every aspect of her life. What distressed her most was that she began to find herself liking the woman, with whom she realized she had much in common. She continued to weep and suffer for many months but the tears were no longer helpless but purposeful. Her initial insane reaction to the loss had eased when she confronted the reality of the other woman and the new tears played an essential part in her healing.

These women and many others behaved in ways that were completely out of character. They sent anonymous letters, day-dreamed about how to damage or poison the other person or find some way of ruining their lives. What is extraordinary is how seldom the anger is unleashed on the partner, the one responsible for the loss. Sometimes women turn their anger against themselves as in the pain of bereavement: take overdoses of sleeping pills, cut their hair short, rake their skin with their finger nails, feeling that physical pain is more tolerable than emotional pain. The tension is most frequently released in tears. Another woman, whose lover went back to his wife, wept herself to sleep every night for six months. Every morning, exhausted but able to cope, she struggled to work. Bitterly ashamed of her failure to hold his love, she couldn't bring herself to discuss what had happened with even her closest friends. She used her weeping time before sleep for long conversations inside her head in which she began to make sense of what had happened.

If we are lucky we have someone in our lives with whom we can shed healing tears. Women are fortunate. They can usually find another woman with whom to share the pain. Men are less fortunate, since they not only have to cope with the cultural fear of showing emotion, but also with the dismissive and often lewd attitudes to women with which they are surrounded. They may find someone to talk to, but rarely someone with whom they can actually cry although Damon Runyan claimed that the tears shed on Broadway by 'guys in love', would produce enough salt water to start an opposition to the Atlantic and the Pacific.

This is why men who have been deeply hurt in an extra marital affair often have a compulsion when it ends to tell all to their wives in a great burst of weeping. The purpose is less to get forgiveness than to get some relief from the tension and the pain. They turn to the one person who may accept their tears without judgement. Some, who may be kinder, will find a way of weeping in their wives' arms without explaining the cause. The wife may have a shrewd idea, but may offer comfort without choosing to seek out the source of the pain.

Shame is at the heart of much of the grieving which women experience when men leave them. Its core is the sense of rejection of the most private and intimate parts of themselves, because that is what women in love offer so generously to men. This is what a girl in Borstal meant when she said to me, 'I gave him everything I had but it wasn't enough'. It's what my friend working in prostitution meant when she said she lost her self-respect when her husband was attracted to her colleague whom she saw as inferior to herself.

Men in love may offer a great deal but they seldom make such a full commitment. They are much more likely to hold on to a degree of independence. This may include the right to give priority to their work, their politics, their hobbies, their nights out with 'the boys'. They seldom give to the relationship the commanding priority that women, particularly in the early stages of loving, feel to be appropriate. The intensity of love which some women feel puzzles many men. Flattered for a little while, they soon begin to feel embarrassed or threatened by the powerful nature of the feeling that surrounds them. It seems to arouse expectations they can't meet, it makes demands on their freedom, they want life to be simpler. For the women on the other hand, this kind of love, if only it could be returned, opens up possibilities of finding a kind of heaven on earth, a healing of past wounds, a gateway into full intimacy with one other person, an end to existential dread and isolation. But it is a great burden to carry, emotionally-demanding, time-consuming and requiring great dedication and understanding of the self and the other. It requires a commitment to the art of loving and experiencing feeling that many women but few men are prepared to make.

It is the same intensity of commitment so many women make to their children, and particularly to their sons. It can be very positive, giving the child a base of confidence from which to move into a creative relationship with the world. It can be destructive as we see in the black humour centring round the image of the Jewish mother who with her tears blackmails her son's emotional life. Such behaviour is not confined to Jewish mothers. It is a temptation for all mothers whose lives are emotionally unfulfilled.

The other side of the story is the pain felt by women when their children suffer, and their bewilderment when that suffering is self-inflicted. I have hanging in my workroom a painting of the Pieta, that powerful image of the dead Christ, taken down from the cross and lying across his mother's lap. It is an image which reminds women that the infant child who once lay comfortably on their lap will grow and suffer. But in my painting, the mother's face is not, as it is in all similar images I have seen, pious and accepting. Rather it looks down at the scarred and broken Christ figure as if to say, 'Why? I carried you in my body for nine months, I loved you and cared for you, why did you do this to yourself?' It is a question many mothers ask as they receive their dead children home from wars, mountain tops and London lavatories where they died of an overdose. These are times when the suffering may be too deep for tears.

5

People, Tears and Institutions

Each man is thrown back on himself alone and there is danger
that he may be shut up in the solitude of his own heart.

Alexis de Tocqueville

The next time you visit your doctor, you might ask to see the buff
envelope which holds your medical history. Printed on it you'll see
a space for the date of birth already filled in and also a space for the
date of death, not yet filled in. The history of your physical and
emotional health lies in that envelope. In due course the information will be processed and used for all kinds of statistical information.

From the day we are born and our births are registered, we are
not only individuals but members of a society which negotiates
with us through institutions. The institutions of health, education
and housing powerfully influence our opportunities and choices in
later life. Others influence the kind of jobs we can get, how much
we'll be paid, how we behave in public (and even in private) and
how we spend our time and money. Some will even try to
influence how we think and feel. Often we don't like them and
when we like them least we call them bureaucracies and feel they
are malignant, that they interfere with our freedoms, that they are
insensitive to our needs. Sometimes this is true. Often we have a
confused feeling that we both need and resent them.

It is the people who work in the institutions who are most
exposed to our dislike. Yet these are the same people who are our
neighbours, our friends and those who sit beside us in the cinema
or at a football ground. So why are they different when met over
the counter in a social security office or a housing department?

Those dealing with the public are usually confronted with
people asking for help. If we are brought up to think of asking for
help as childish, and if our own requests for help have not been

80

swiftly and cheerfully met, we are less likely to respond in a simple and positive way to demands. If in addition we have been brought up in the tradition that to show feeling is a vulgar and lower-class way of behaving, we will seek to drain it out of any situations in which we are involved. The civil service and institutions based on this style see feeling as irrelevant in work performance. It is a dangerous complication which must be filtered out. Rules, logic and reason are the principles which govern. Many would agree but this system ignores the customers who may be full of emotions like fear and helplessness. If ignored, these feelings turn to tears or anger.

Our institutions were set up by middle-class people and the staff, even when their own origins are working-class, reflect those values. When customers express feelings, certain behaviour like shouting or swearing is seen as 'low-class' and treated with contempt as 'ignorant'. Those who manage to present themselves with a cool, unemotional middle-class style have a better chance of their messages being responded to. Some social workers try to teach their own customers some codes to use when speaking to a doctor or a magistrate or an official in the housing department.

Some cultures – the Afro-Caribbean is one – allow much more open expression of all emotions, laughter, grief and tears. Some working-class groups are the same, able to have a knees-up in a pub, sing in a bus or appear on panel games on television in which they laugh loudly, show disappointment openly and accept the idea that luck is more important than knowledge. The middle-class panel game 'Mastermind' demonstrates a rather different view of the world, much more low-key, but much more effective in gaining social respect and status.

Middle- or upper-class grief is hidden under controlled facial muscles or even under a black veil, as with members of the royal family. It is as if to let people see your feelings takes away some of your power. But at regularly photographed IRA or UDI funerals, or those of victims of tragedies, grieving working-class women are shown with their mouths open, weeping, their bodies distorted with grief, part of a more ancient tradition. Working-class parents whose children are missing or have been murdered will appear on television asking for help. They weep openly and harrowingly, unlike middle-class parents who are seldom willing to appear, seeing their grief as more private. *Each of us lies somewhere on a spectrum of ability to show feeling which is reflected in our behaviour. This is often closely related to where we see ourselves on the spectrum of social class.*

In approaching institutions for help, the appearance of subservience can help people who are clearly powerless. But it may be difficult for some people to pretend when they are overwhelmed with anger. Tears are a two-edged weapon when dealing with officials who may be embarrassed by them. If the official is a man who is uncomfortable when his wife cries or a woman ill-at-ease with her own tears, the weeping customer can seem very threatening.

Some institutions, like the Department of Social Security section which deals with non-contributory benefits, are in a particularly sensitive relationship with the public. Their customers often come to them under considerable stress, dependent, short of money, embarrassed and afraid of rejection. They have waited in an unattractive waiting room for long periods and by the time they reach a counter are at breaking-point. The official may be equally under stress, overworked, resentful and conscious that the administrative back-up of the office is not very efficient. In this kind of situation neither can say what their real feelings are. A true conversation might be,

'I am needing help. Are you willing to help me?'
'I can't bear anyone asking me for help. Who is willing to help *me*'?.

But these words are never said. Two needy people in competition for caring are more likely to end up bitter, hostile and dissatisfied, when what they most need to do is weep on each other's shoulders. But that thought is not to be tolerated. The applicant goes away complaining vehemently about the treatment received, the official retires behind the partition to complain about yet another bad-tempered, ungrateful recipient of state benefits.

Since officials and clerks are not allowed to express their real feelings at work, it is not surprising that they have difficulty tolerating the feelings of their customers. Any member of staff who sat down at his or her desk and wept with sorrow at the pain they are constantly having to encounter in their customers' lives, anyone who wept with frustration at their helplessness in the face of the world suffering that they perceive would be considered mentally unstable. The entire structure depends on denial of pain in the person with whom they are dealing. Their judgement might be affected. A nineteenth-century Rothschild is reported as saying, 'Throw out that beggar, he's breaking my heart'. Any sensitive bank manager must have the same feeling. This denial of pain extends to all aspects of life within the work place. If their own heart is breaking it should not be allowed to show. A parent might be dying of cancer, a love affair might have ended ... the pain must not be allowed to leak out.

Some organizations now insist that their staff be constantly cheerful and smiling, no matter how they feel. Staff working the tills in supermarkets are being told that they must smile as they check out each item and present the bill. Human beings are expected to be as mechanical as the musak. Within limits this seems a not unreasonable request. In Marks and Spencers, as you make your way out of the staff area into the shop, a notice greets you, 'Smile, you are now entering the public area'. But Marks and Spencers have a reputation for good employer/employee relationships. Their staff have good conditions of service and have an inner motivation to relate pleasantly to their customers.

It can be a different matter where staff are overworked and underpaid and still expected to smile constantly. It comes close to what Arthur Haley described in his novel *Roots*. There the black slaves, no matter how angry or unhappy they felt, as soon as a white man approached began to shuffle and smile so as to look harmless and contented. Not to do so could result in a beating. Will we see women working on check out tills being sacked because they cannot keep a smile screwed on to their faces for eight hours every day? This insistence on 'a brave face' presents particular hazards for working women, who have traditionally been allowed more public expression of feeling than men. They have to learn in competing with men for recognition and promotion to suppress any signs of feminine 'weakness'. Tears must not be allowed to fill their eyes and under no circumstances run down their cheeks. The male mafia will close ranks and deem such a woman unstable, neurotic and quite unsuitable for responsibility. If she has a male boss who has tantrums that would be more appropriate in a three-year-old, a boss who shouts at and bullies her, in the institutional world of male values, she will lose all respect if she cries. She may know that her tears will relieve her tension more effectively than shouting back or pretending not to notice, or they may be tears of anger rather than the vulnerability so despised by her colleagues. Nor will concession be made to a tendency to weep during the days immediately before her period. To draw attention to that would compound the woman's error. The mask she has to wear in order to be accepted as an equal is seen to be seriously flawed.

The problem for women is highlighted by a thirty-year-old trainee RSPCA inspector, dismissed because she wept when dogs were put to death. She appealed against her dismissal under the Sex Discrimination Act but lost her case. Mary Warnock, the philosopher, argued that the dismissal was justified since professionals must learn to face a work demand like mercy killing with calm, although not necessarily with indifference. She thought it very bad for the image of women that they should always be seen as the people most likely to follow their hearts and not their heads. Women, she argued, should practise not crying except in exceptionally worthy circumstances. Those tears, which led to dismissal, could have been seen as a source of energy and redirected by an understanding supervisor to a powerful commitment to doing the work well. She might still have shed a few tears when the dogs were put down but those tears could have represented a fitting tribute of respect to lovely creatures whom human beings treat so shabbily. I would rather have an RSPCA worker who retained the capacity to weep than one hardened to the darker necessities of the job.

Geraldine Bedell, writing in the *Independent* newspaper, described what happened when the senior partner of a law firm was confronted with tears from an exhausted female at the end of a marathon deal. 'How can I ever treat her quite the same again', he said. 'There's always this fear she won't be able to cope, so you don't give her the difficult jobs'. She describes another incident where a woman, reduced to tears by a senior colleague, began to realize that he was enjoying seeing her cry. Bedell quotes Coral Morgan Thomson, a director of Role Management, a company which specializes in stress counselling for executives. She believes it is the 'fundamentally weedy' men who like to see women cry, and it is assertive women they attack because they are afraid of them. Bedell goes on to say that when a man embarks on one of those humiliation rituals which men behind desks have been perfecting for generations, she wishes she had the guts to introduce a bit of power play and weep gently but composedly. 'Why', she asks, 'give up this healthy show of emotion for heart attacks?'

But many men are genuinely afraid of tears. Some are afraid of their own tears and the abyss that would open in their lives if they once allowed themselves to make contact with their own pain. For others, seeing a woman cry revives hidden feelings of seeing their mothers cry. Those memories cover very complicated feelings of helplessness, the awfulness of seeing the most important person, whom you depend on for protection, in acute distress. Colin White, in a cartoon, shows a woman weeping copiously over a man at a desk who is hiding behind an umbrella and waving a white flag.

There may be feelings of anger against the person who caused a woman to cry. In his book on Maxwell, Joe Haines describes how Maxwell's normally imperturbable secretary burst into tears after a spell of work when he had been even more demanding than usual. He walked into her office and found her crying. 'Who's done that to you?' he demanded angrily. 'I'll sack him!'

As women return to work in institutions after child-bearing, they perform extraordinary emotional gymnastics. In their daily lives with children they engage freely and fully in fundamental feelings of love, anger, frustration, fury, pain and joy often coupled with tears. They learn to do several things at once, they use skills with their children of conciliation, negotiation, contract. They recognize the pointlessness of confrontation with a small creature who doesn't understand the assumptions on which the adult is operating, and develop a capacity to catch the passing joy and respect serendipity. They know how helpful tears are to defuse tension and how constructive their aftermath can be. The healing quality of tears and laughter is part of their lives.

None of these skills are recognized by their male colleagues in the workplace. Accordingly, women may abandon them and try to fit into institutional patterns which make no sense to them but which they are constantly assured are superior. Others may use what they have learned to 'handle' male colleagues but few are able to influence the masculine value base of their work places. These are some of the reasons that women are often happier working together and reluctant to fight their way into senior management. They reject a driven competitive style which sacrifices family and fun. We are learning that the way institutions are organized is increasingly a problem for men as well as women. Institutions which concede no place for feelings and assume that the two aspects of our lives, private and public, have to be kept absolutely separate, are not healthy for anyone.

But those of us who deal with bureaucratic institutions simply as part of normal life, while we may find it frustrating, even demeaning, can at least retreat into the private institutions of our family where, if we are lucky, we will find acceptance, support and warmth. This does not apply to those people who spend long periods of time in institutions which they are powerless to leave and with little or no freedom of choice ... children's homes, boarding schools, prisons, mental hospitals, homes for people with disabilities. Some children brought up in institutions are so damaged by these experiences that they cannot live in a family where they have to respond to others' feelings and may escape into work in an institutional setting. They are particularly unable to cope with the intimacy of marriage and, if bewildered by their spouse's demands, may flare into violence.

What the institutional life does well, if backed up by economic stability or an ideological message, is produce people who cope well in situations where feelings can be a handicap to efficient functioning. The kibbutz child does well in the army and is comfortable living in a group; the man reared in middle-class boarding schools and residential colleges learns skills of suppressing emotion, and develops attitudes of tolerance and a capacity to work productively with others whom he may not like.

People like this are valuable to the civil service and other bureaucratic organizations. The British Empire was built on the unshed tears of small boys in preparatory and public schools. It was a terrible price to pay but most defend the legacy of ideas of fairness, justice and good government they communicated to many parts of the globe. This system has also produced a remarkable number of idiosyncratic and creative characters who have transcended the rigidity of the system and transformed their pain into poetry, music and literature.

We can now go on to look at two very different institutions, one socially acceptable, the other not, in order to see the extent to which they allow the expression of distress through tears.

TEARS AND HOSPITALS

... to some people, especially those vulnerable to fear and to pain, there sometimes seems no refuge, no support. Hospital staff rush here and there, tell them to wait, to walk down long forbidding corridors to see a doctor – whose name they haven't even been told – who may not even speak to them by name in a way they can understand.

A receptionist in a new, busy and large district hospital.

In this country a hospital accepts and cares for any person who cannot be cared for in their own home, but to step into their admission halls is not always the loving experience needed. Few people complain. How could they? When our bodies fail us we feel panic and helplessness. It is a fundamental source of human suffering.

When healthy we are able to look with a cool eye at what medicine offers; when we're ill, we become like frightened children looking at mother and father to make us better. When we are so ill that we have to stay in bed and be looked after, we are driven back even further into unconscious memories of having to call or cry for help for even the simplest needs.

We have been taught that the only solution for us is to take our sick body to a doctor who will make decisions about it, an all-powerful doctor who carries our life or death within his hands. No hospital can function well without receptionists, cleaners, administrators, porters and all the other ancillary staff. But for patients, in the moment of need, the most important people are those who lay hands on them and have power over them ... doctors and nurses.

Stephani Cook, writing about her experiences in hospital, describes how when told that she had to have yet another in a series of operations, describes how she cried like a child:

... unashamedly, loudly, wetly – as spasm after spasm of misery washed over me. What would happen to me? What would become of me? What had I done? Why didn't it stop? Nobody seemed to be in control ... All these big, strong, wise doctors were supposed to be in charge, they were supposed to be helping me – that was the only compensation for the humiliating procedure I'd had to endure.

Hospital doctors, with some marvellous exceptions, have clung to old patterns of training where the doctor protected himself from the patient's feelings of panic and terror in the face of illness and death. Medical students who fail to do this, who show their own distress and pain at the plight of the patient, are identified as unsuitable or unprofessional and expected to 'harden up'. Many protect themselves even from patients' questions, by always being very busy or emotionally unapproachable. Patients, particularly women who are conditioned from childhood to be accepting rather than questioning, are given the sense that they mustn't try to invade medical territory.

As long as doctors hold on to the role of being omnipotent, it is not surprising they need defences. It is a great burden for them if they cannot share their uncertainty in the face of a complicated diagnosis, or their distress if they have to predict an inevitable death or permanent disability. An oncologist may have to diagnose a malignant tumour several times a day, an opthalmologist may have to tell five patients, in the one day, that they are going blind. In any out-patient department patients are daily being given life-or-death judgements about their future.

The attitude of the doctors then usually forces patients to conceal their spontaneous feelings about the information. Any whose feelings overflow are liable to be seen as weak or 'difficult'. 'Courage' is the response that is admired. It appears to make life easier for everyone. One young man, a student, given such a diagnosis wrote privately about that experience:

> The 'something' in my chest had been identified. I was told I wouldn't be fit enough to go to college. What was I to do? Was the next year to be filled by more unemployment and more chemotherapy? The future seemed empty. What was it to be filled by? The news had been given clearly and simply. 'All right? Do you understand? Any questions?' I nodded and said 'Yes' and 'No' in reply. I wanted to cry there and then but I was in the ward surrounded by people who would want to dam up my tears, so I stood up, put my jacket on and walked out.
>
> I found myself somewhere quiet. As I sat there I recalled the words the Doctor had just spoken to me and the tears came back. This time I didn't stop them. I sat feeling his words and the tears came faster and faster, but then without noticing I stopped feeling his words and thought of their meaning. And as I

thought about their meaning, the tears slowed down until they stopped. I had received bad news. I cried because of it, but the time comes when crying stops. It's not a forced ending, but natural.

So my tears have fallen. They have fallen since and they'll fall again. They have fallen fast and slowly. They have fallen with anger and sadness. Sometimes they've been bitter and sometimes hopeless, but no matter how they've fallen or why they've fallen, the time comes when they stop and whether you like it or not, or intend it or not, stop they do.

He died a year later. It is good to know that he was able to share his tears with the hospital chaplain.

I asked an eye specialist, a thoughtful and genuinely caring man, how patients responded to going blind. 'Do they cry?', I asked him. 'They probably do', he said, 'but I can't let them cry with me when I've got a queue of people'. I tried to find out if there was any place in the hospital where they could have gone to weep and share their distress. There was no such refuge that he knew of. It may have had to be a lavatory or else the bus on the way home. Most hospitals now have chapels, but many are hidden down corridors and are uninviting.

The most common defence against feeling for hospital doctors is to see the symptom but not the patient. A friend of mine, admitted for investigation of a lump in her breast, refused to give automatic permission for a mastectomy. On his next ward round the surgeon said, 'What's all this about? After all at your age you're not going to need your breast any more.' She was a very attractive, unmarried woman of forty-one. Controlling her anger, she looked at him and said, 'You're older than me. Do you want to keep your testicles'? He swept away and she never saw him again in the hospital. Six months later, having kept her breast intact, she was at a party when the surgeon appeared on the other side of the room. She made her way over to him. He had no recollection of her and began to flirt mildly. Not being a woman to miss an opportunity, she described their previous meeting. Sadly he didn't appreciate the joke and left the party early.

Not all women are as strong-minded as my friend. Stories brought back from gynaecological examinations and procedures carried out by male doctors are at best disturbing, at worst horrifying. It is common to feel treated as an object. Comments are made to the perineum rather than the person. Expressions of pain as the examination takes place rouse irritation or accusations of neurosis. Many women must have wondered how men would cope if the same scraping and probing techniques were carried out routinely on male genitalia. One woman writing anonymously to a women's magazine told of her distress at a particularly dehumanizing gynaecological examination. The nurse was aware of her humiliation and kept throwing sympathetic glances. She finished her letter by saying that this must seem a very small matter to people suffering serious illnesses but she resented not feeling able to complain because of her fear of being seen as childish or neurotic. As happens with children, her pain was compounded by being made to feel ashamed.

The greatest problem, particularly for surgeons, is the patient whom an operation has not helped and who is now dying. There seems to be no place for a dying person on the surgical wards. It is almost as if having failed, the surgical staff cannot bear to see the patient. It is too great a challenge to their image of themselves as healers. They are trained only to cure, to treat and to prolong life. They are taught nothing about helping people to die. Their response is sometimes brutal. It was made clear to a friend of mine who was dying that he was not wanted on the ward, not through words but by the minimum care he was given after an unsuccessful operation and the refusal of any doctor to speak to him. He knew that staff were avoiding him. His wife was asked, by a junior consultant who could give no information about the operation and its results, to take him home. She is herself a nurse, not by any means inarticulate, but she could get no one to speak to or to tell her anything. She described it as a nightmare. Ultimately her GP intervened and was told that the outlook was hopeless. He persuaded her to bring her husband home, where he died within a few weeks.

One of the most distressing factors is the 'jollying up' attitude of staff and their expectations that the patients and their families will collude with the ritual pretence that everything is for the best in this best of all possible worlds. A pregnant woman whose baby had died in the womb was not told that her baby was dead until after it was born. The staff thought it better to let her go through her labour cheerfully. One nurse described how she always knocks at the door of a private room if there is a terminally ill patient in case she should catch them crying. 'I don't want to embarrass them'.

Roehampton Hospital is, justly, world-famous for its marvellous skills of rehabilitation for people with limb disabilities. But patients say that in the course of treatment, they are never permitted to express tearfulness or despair. A relentless cheerfulness and optimism is demanded. For some patients this seems superficially to be effective, but for men or women whose background or culture more readily allows them to express feeling, this is very difficult. To be accepted they are forced to develop if not actual defences, then masks against the external world.

Beata Bishop in her book *A Time to Heal*, which describes her experience of cancer and how she ultimately cured it by using alternative healing methods, writes of her first experience of conventional surgery. After the operation, her surgeon dropped in to see her every day, often twice a day. She remembers it in this way,

> Looking back, I find it interesting that our exchanges were consistently humorous, as if we had been rehearsing for a Wit and Wisdom contest. I was acting out the role of the good, courageous patient as I saw it at the time, while Mr Lennox was no doubt pleased to find me co-operative, free from despair and, above all, unemotional. I played his game and he rewarded me with encouraging remarks about my cancer-free future.

Even while this game was being played out, Beata Bishop knew intuitively that she was not cured, had yet to experience the dark part of the cycle of her illness and 'should not pretend that it was, in fact, light'. The cancer re-emerged in her groin within a year. She went into the darkness of that experience, found within herself a healing power which she allied with alternative therapies and is now fully cured.

None of this behaviour adopted by professionals is intended to be unhelpful. The rationalization is that everything is done in the interests of the patient, but it is also designed to protect professionals from feelings that are, for them, genuinely intolerable. The rationalization is that it helps patients. The reality is that it doesn't. What the patients need is to have emotional fear and pain acknowledged and expressed through words, tears or in whatever other way they find helpful.

On the hospital wards, nurses have most physical contact with patients. They wash them, help them perform the intimate functions of relieving bladder and bowels, change dressings on wounds, give medicine, help them take their first steps after an operation, make beds, waken them up, tell them to go to sleep, close their eyes when they die. They become the parent, the patient the helpless and often frightened child.

Nurses are directly confronted with the reality of suffering, with the fragility of human experience, in ways that few other people, even doctors, know. They see not only the immediacy of pain but the effects of damage, accident and fate on human lives. Their work involves tasks which most people find distasteful or frightening – from emptying bed pans, giving enemas, changing dressings on sometimes horrific wounds, to laying out and washing the dead. Their work arouses strong feelings, sometimes mixed and confused, feelings of compassion, disgust, anger, fear and anxiety. They may be aroused sexually by the naked bodies they wash and care for. They may resent patients who rouse these confused feelings. When they are tired, exhausted or not feeling well they may envy patients the care they give them. They have to be the good mother, when they themselves may need mothering.

They also deal with the anxieties and guilt of relatives. It is the doctor's job to tell the patient or the patient's family, when he or she is terminally ill, but once the diagnosis and prognosis have been given, the nurse copes with the emotional effects. She has probably known what the doctor is going to say and may feel she has betrayed the family or patient and her relationship with them by not previously telling them the truth. If the relationship has been real, she will have her own grief and difficulty in coping with the diagnosis, as well as her own anger at the surgeon or the doctor. Her feelings may be complex.

Most nurses are first thrown into these situations at around eighteen years of age, before they have an opportunity to sort out the demands of their own emotional lives. They come to the job with vague convictions of wanting to care for people, of doing a worthwhile job for which they will be given respect. It is important to see themselves as 'good' people. To come to terms with the maelstrom of feelings aroused would mean accepting what most have been taught are 'wrong' feelings for a 'nice' person to have.

As with doctors, there are always nurses whose personal strengths are such that they can openly and lovingly respond to a patient's pain, grief and distress without needing defences. Stephani Cook described one such encounter when at the limits of her courage:

What a relief to be able to complain ... openly, ... freely, to say how I really feel! [She] ... will not interpret my sharing of my pain as an assault, she will not turn away or urge me to be strong, or murmur some expression of sympathy or swallow hard because there is, finally, nothing to say to someone who is beyond comfort though not beyond caring.

One way of avoiding anxiety is not to be constantly reminded of individuals. Talking about the patient as 'the spleen in bed 9', or 'the appendicitis in the corner', or in a maternity unit calling everyone 'Mother' removes individual characteristics, neutralizes them and protects the nurse from emotional demands. Life is particularly hard for nurses on children's wards where the emotional demands can be overwhelming.

A nurse has to learn to control the show of feeling and avoid emotional involvement with the patient. It is an important protection against behaving in unprofessional ways like procuring an illegal abortion or killing a handicapped baby. In the past this aspect of training has been overemphasized but efforts are now made to strike a better balance. Administrative techniques like splitting up contact with patients into ritual tasks, or moving staff from ward to ward, are now questioned.

We know that the patient who can show distress about their condition, talk about it and share anxiety has a much faster recovery rate than one who suppresses such feelings. Alexander the Great knew this intuitively when, himself having been wounded in the thigh, he walked round his wounded men and asked each to talk about his experience in the battle and how his wound had been received. This is particularly the case for patients undergoing operations. The work of psychiatrists such as Maxwell Jones, who established the first therapeutic community, shows that the nurse who is given time to talk with and listen to patients is a most potent healing force for the human spirit. These practices are being used in marvellous ways in hospices for the dying, both in the independent sector and in the National Health Service. They offer great hope. We need now to transfer this quality of under-standing of human need to general hospitals.

For several years a new model for nursing has been researched, written about and tried out which allocates a number of patients rather than tasks to each nurse. Their role is then to help the patient to meet and fulfil the 'activities of daily living'. They prepare individual care-plans for each patient with goals and objectives to be drawn up and revised by both the nurse and the patient. But if there aren't enough staff to meet this approach, the result is a double stress for the nurse who is taught such an approach, but given no opportunity to put it into practice. In most training schools little or no individual emotional support is avail-able. The pressure is inevitably on getting the nursing techniques 'right'. The massive anxiety aroused by these conflicts has to be resolved, or else the nurse will either drop out of training as a 'failure', or resolve the conflict by reverting to defensive techni-ques.

Most patients can cope with unacknowledged grief and anxiety because they are in hospital for a short time. But there are chronic conditions which mean longer stays. A friend of mine visiting a hospital saw an elderly man wandering around and crying. A nurse was scolding him and telling him to sit down and be quiet. On being asked what was wrong, she explained that his wife, on an adjacent ward, had died the previous day. Perhaps, the visitor suggested, he wants to go to her locker, go through her things, handle them. 'The locker's been cleared', she said. 'There's a new patient in that bed'. In this same hospital, when relatives come to the mortuary to visit the dead member of their family, they view them through a sheet of glass. They are given no opportunity to touch the dead person or put something – a flower, a crucifix – into their hand to take to the grave. The practice started when post-mortems were more common than now and the intention was to protect the 'outsider' from the smell. But it still carries on and with it the denial of mortality and humanity.

Chris Heginbotham, when director of *Mind*, wrote of one sight he had witnessed in one well-known hospital south-east of London:

> I came across one of the most pitiful things I have ever known. This was a man in his late 50s or early 60s, living on a ward with thirty other men. There was no privacy, the 'moving wallpaper'

simply ran from the time they returned from industrial therapy to tea-and-bed time at about 9.15p.m. Indeed, the sound of the tea trolley created a Pavlovian reaction among the 30 men. Some in pyjamas, others half dressed suddenly lined up to take their tea and pills.

The man I am talking about got up slowly. He was known to abscond from the ward – this was a bit of a nuisance as there were only two nursing staff on duty at any one time. Recently he had had to have a catheter fitted for some medical problem and because of his absconding behaviour, the nurses had hit on a really original wheeze – to force him to carry the slowly filling urine bag in one of those four-milk crates one sometimes sees on doorsteps. Short of outright brutality that is probably one of the most degrading things you can do to a person.

People who are mentally ill, mentally handicapped or old are the most vulnerable. It is assumed, quite incorrectly, that they have no feelings. Staff shortages, combined with the patients' helplessness and their invisibility from the general public (few visitors come to these wards), make it easy for private toiletting or modesty to be ignored and emotional lives denied. The patients' response is to behave like automata; awareness of their pain would be unbearable. Cuts in the amount of money spent on direct services to patients as opposed to buildings mean that in wards where few staff members care for a large number of patients standards of care fall well below tolerable levels. Wards smell of urine and faeces, incontinent patients may be left unattended for hours – even fed while sitting in their excrement. Staff who are overworked and overstressed may react to patients' demands with anger or violence. Everyone's standards of behaviour deteriorate so that all personal dignity evaporates. Both staff and patients are brutalized, locked in an intolerable embrace.

In the general hospital, where visitors pour through every day of the week, physical humiliation is less likely though ward rounds by some consultants are still an exercise in treating the patient as a malfunctioning piece of machinery. It is in the outpatient department that many people feel particularly vulnerable as they wait in a cubicle, wearing paper gowns with no idea of what is happening, as staff rush around self-consciously doing more important things than talking to a patient.

One group of workers who often catch the backlog of feelings not allowed on the wards are physiotherapists. The whole process of massage involves yielding to another's care. It rouses far-off memories of infancy, of being handled and given comfort. It is not surprising that a high proportion of patients burst into tears as soon as the physiotherapist begins work. Sometimes the patient will talk, pouring out problems and anxieties, but more often nothing is said and tears slowly subside into relaxation. Some physiotherapists have intuitively incorporated this response into their work. In one sophisticated Scottish mental hospital the nursing staff have learned to refer patients with whom they are failing to communicate to the physiotherapist. These are patients cut off from their capacity to feel, presumably to protect themselves from emotional pain. Frequently, when they feel the physiotherapist's hands on them they will begin to cry. The massage is not stopped, even to produce a handkerchief, and no reference is made to the cause of the tears. Before the patient leaves the physiotherapist uses a particular technique which helps work through the big sobs that so often follow crying, believing that the crying has used up oxygen and big sobs restore balance. Before the patients go back to the ward, they will pat their faces back into place and often ask for reassurance that no-one will be told. This is a desperate comment on the forbidden nature of tears.

Social workers and chaplains, with a hospital office, also offer opportunities for a few patients to weep and express distress in privacy, in a sympathetic atmosphere. But important though these opportunities are to individuals, they are marginal to the life of the hospital. One most distressing aspect of all institutions is the lack of privacy. If you're a patient on a ward, where can you cry? There is no place where you can be quiet with a partner or a friend. About the only place is the lavatory and in the lavatory you cry alone. How does it make someone like a woman who has just had an abortion feel having to go to a lavatory to express her grief in tears? A natural and innocent experience like weeping becomes sullied and distorted. When respect is not given to our tears we are denied the relief they can bring.

TEARS AND PRISONS

> *But there is no sleep when men must weep*
> *who never yet have wept.*
> Oscar Wilde, 'The Ballad of Reading Gaol'.

Something was thrown into her cell.

'Have a cigarette', the kid said. 'It helps. Stops you from crying'.

She saw a box of cigarettes with matches tucked into the wrapper. So she was still crying. She hadn't realized that . . .

'The thing about it is', the fellow said, 'you have to take a deep breath to light up, and that does it, that stops the crying.' . . .

She inhaled deeply. He was right. She had stopped crying. She felt better, too, toughened, more in command. As soon as she exhaled, she inhaled again.

'It's a very simple theory', the fellow said. 'It's impossible to cry and inhale at the same time. You'd choke. It works like a charm. Some people sing, whistle, talk – that blocks off the crying mechanism too.'

She nodded.

'You latch on to these techniques after you've been around a bit', he said . . . 'I've been in and out of a lot of jails in my time.'

Helen Yglesias, *Sweetsir.*

Sometimes, when driving through a strange place, usually on the outskirts of a town, I see a building immediately recognizable as a prison. As I look, I half expect to see the air above the building turbulent and violent with the compressed energy of the pain and anger held there. Prisons are terrible places. No matter how they are dressed up, modernized or staffed by well-meaning people, there is not a single prison in Britain that we can or should be proud of. Indeed, we should ask forgiveness of everyone held there.

It is made clear to the prisoner from the moment he sets foot in the institution that his personal feelings are considered irrelevant. He is given a number, stripped of all personal possessions, made to shower and wash his hair and body with a lice-killing soap and then given uniform clothing. He has to respond like a well-trained dog to demands shouted at him. The small cubicle in which he has to strip, hand over his own clothes and don prison uniform is known as the 'dog box'. No matter what difficulties he encounters within the system, he can expect no sympathy. His progress is assessed on his ability to respond promptly and without feeling to whatever is asked.

Prisons, as we know them, are fairly modern institutions. In earlier, less complicated times an offender might be banished, mutilated or hanged. Justice was dispensed in a summary way.

Prisons were only used to hold a few people until trial. Now they hold tens of thousands.

Every process of the criminal justice system, even before a sentence is passed and guilt or innocence established, is designed to humiliate and intimidate the person being held or questioned. If a sentence of imprisonment is passed the process is intensified. The object is for the institution to establish, as quickly as possible, its power over the inmate. This was shown in its most brutal form in a report published following riots in an Australian prison. An initiation for prisoners had been established where for the first week officers were encouraged to violently beat and humiliate the new prisoner in nauseous ways. Only after his spirit had been broken did the brutality ease up. He was then 'manageable'. This kind of procedure may work with the majority but the marvellous thing about human beings is that there are always some not subdued. We applaud this kind of person when they climb mountains, cross deserts, sail oceans and survive against incredible odds. It is precisely the same quality that makes them resist brutality in prisons but we do not applaud that. In the Australian prison the inmates succeeded in setting their buildings on fire, an act which led to the enquiry and the report. An Australian judge, a passionate advocate of the human spirit, has a photograph of the prison burning hanging on his office wall. It reinforces his faith in human beings.

The ideal prisoner is not a human being but an automaton who will respond immediately to orders, eat when they're told to, work, take exercise, sleep, and in all circumstances be respectful to authority. Preferably he should not show any feelings; almost the only one considered 'respectable' for male prisoners is anger. Anger is understood in these all-male institutions by both staff and prisoners. Within reason they are all comfortable with it. Subservience is also shown because other prisoners see it as a mask, necessary for survival for weaker or less competent prisoners. Away from the staff, the subservient prisoner will say what he really thinks. The truly subservient prisoner is respected by no-one, staff or inmates. No one will cry openly.

The prison hero is the one who most openly shows anger and contempt for the staff. Equally, the most brutal and aggressive member of staff is often most admired by the inmates as well as being most deeply hated. Staff and inmates meet in a culture of machismo, of men being tough. Normally senior staff have become separated from this but their own experience in the ranks (if they had any) leaves them fully aware of the emotional dynamics between landing staff and prisoners. Occasionally they are unable to leave it behind.

One story now in the mythology of the prison service concerns a governor who granted an interview to a prisoner but rather summarily refused his request. He was suddenly attacked by the prisoner with a knife specially sharpened for the purpose. The officers guarding him stopped him reaching the governor just in time. Instead of putting him on a charge, the governor took the knife out of his hand and, while the prisoner was still being held by the officers, slashed his face. It was done, the story goes, coolly and without malice. The governor became a hero to many of his staff and prisoners, including the one slashed. They admired him even as they reviled him. Psychologically there may be little difference between the personalities of some staff and prisoners. Their different paths can seem as much the result of luck, accident or opportunity as any capacity to distinguish between right and wrong.

Since anger is the only respected currency, it becomes extraordinarily difficult for genuine feelings of distress or even sorrow to be expressed by prisoners. A frequent comment of observers about a prisoner in for a serious offence like murder is that he shows no remorse. This becomes particularly important when the staff are writing reports for the parole board. A desperate prisoner, knowing perfectly well what is expected of him may well offer to a chaplain or prison visitor any amount of repentance; he might even undertake a religious conversion. But the prisoner who feels integrity and a sense of loyalty to his own group, although he may sincerely repent his crime, might find it difficult to express this publicly. The whole atmosphere discourages sharing one's more personal feelings.

If prisoners feel they are treated as less than human, without normal instincts of tenderness or capacity for pain, they react as if that is the case. Pain cannot be contained indefinitely within the person. It has to leak out. In prison it leaks out in anger and displays of violence either between the prisoners or against the staff. This is true both for individuals and groups. What are seen by the public as the most depraved of men still have profound needs to express their sorrow even when, with the most damaged people, it seems to lie too deep for tears. St Francis of Assisi wrote about the 'gift of tears', but it was Denis Nilson, a mass murderer who couldn't cry, who wrote 'It must be the most wonderful gift to be able to throw your arms around someone and just weep'. If that opportunity had been available to him, who knows what difference it might have made?

But to cry in a setting which allows no privacy is difficult. The majority share a cell; not even the lavatories are private. A telephone message may have come to say that a parent has died, a letter saying that a wife is seeking a divorce, but there is nowhere to hide and be alone with sorrow. Indeed, men are not allowed to display any tender feelings under any circumstances. Some have been known to shed tears of repentance as part of an experience of religious conversion, and refuge may be found in the brief visits of the chaplain. This is not always greeted with respect by other inmates or by staff. This denial of feeling is not difficult to achieve. A very high proportion of prisoners come from a background of grossly limited educational and economic opportunity. Before reaching the status of adult prisoner, many have trod a path of minor delinquency which involved time spent in residential care. These junior institutions are the preparatory schools of the prisons, not because they train criminals, but because they train youngsters to cope with a regime which denies tenderness, warmth and the right to weep with and for your own pain.

This style fits too well into the values and expectations most will have encountered from male relatives and heroes. 'Real' men in the world of the socially deprived don't show feelings, especially feelings of tenderness or tearfulness, in public. What is allowed is sentimentality in drunken songs of nationality and ideal love. Mawkish videos are legitimate triggers for a show of feeling. Many of the men in prison have poured their frustrated tenderness onto small children, and this is one reason why offenders against children receive such short shrift.

In prisons which offer art or creative writing classes, inmates will pour out their frustrated feelings in painting or poetry. This kind of activity is seen as marginal to the work of the prison instead of as a central opportunity to reawaken feelings and capacities which have been stunted. The Special Unit in Barlinnie Prison has showed dramatically how powerful the influence of art can be.

Instead of prison being used, as it could be, as a living and learning centre for human relationships, prisoners are savagely taught that it is dangerous to let your feelings be seen because they can be used against you. Hostile staff or fellow prisoners are known to use the technique of 'winding you up' to force a display of feeling, which is then punished or ridiculed.

Each experience of imprisonment, for even the most hardened recidivist, is, until the routine is established which numbs the mind, a wrenching of the spirit. Except for those few unhappy souls who have so lost their emotional capacities that they are grateful to have all choice removed from their lives, each person who hears the prison door clang feels a desolation at being cut off from the life of the world and from those they love. Sadness at the loss, and anger against those who, as they see it, have deprived them of liberty – the police, the judge, the prison staff – war within the soul. The sadness cannot be shown. Here all the valued qualities are of being a 'real' man, a 'hard' man. If 'big boys don't cry', then male prisoners certainly can't. The fact that you're frightened (and many men in prison have good cause to be frightened, either of violence from other prisoners and staff or else of homosexual demands) cannot be shown. If you show it you're finished, without respect from your peers and always an underdog. The prisoner learns in this jungle to trust no one, and because no one is to be trusted then it becomes additionally dangerous to share feelings because you never know when they will be used against you. Staff, learning of some intimate aspect of a prisoner's life, perhaps from seeing a file or overhearing a chaplain or social worker discuss confidential information, would be expected to use it to put the prisoner down.

Those who suffer most are the prisoners who allow their mask to sink through all the layers of their personality and blot out the warm, loving, sorrowing parts of themselves. They will say that they don't have the courage to stay emotionally alive, particularly if they are serving a long sentence. Some refuse to allow visits from their wives; they will say they don't want letters, to be reminded of birthdays, nor sent a Christmas card. They would rather play dead than face the pain of thinking about their wives and family and the ordinary small activities of family life which they didn't sufficiently value when they had freedom. There are other pains too, such as celibacy. Outside people talk about prisoners missing physical sex and the need for conjugal visits as if they were just animals who needed relief from tension. It is true that most prisoners miss sexual contact but not just to get relief. Masturbation is freely practiced, even in cells shared by three men and usually homosexual encounters are possible, but the real loss is not genital sex but the small intimacies that freedom makes possible . . . the hugging, the kissing, the cuddling, the skin contact, the smell not only of their woman but of their children after a bath.

And there is the pain of jealousy. The agony of lying locked in a cell and wondering what your wife or girl friend is doing, with whom and to whom. Imagination runs riot, memories of one's own lovemaking being replayed with another man playing your part. Masturbation using your own woman in your imagination turns into a nightmare if these other thoughts intrude, and if you carry these thoughts all week and then allow her to visit, you may fail when talking to her to distinguish between reality and fantasy and ruin the visit for both of you. How much easier to cut yourself off from all these problems and withdraw emotionally into the less demanding machine of prison life. One prisoner put it like this: 'I waken up every morning with this pain. It's terrible. It's not that I want to die, but I just want to get out of my mind'. He means this literally.

It is this wanting to get out of one's mind that creates such a strong demand for drugs in prisons. They ease the pain, creating a private world of peace into which the prisoner can withdraw and temporarily forget the awfulness. Some patients who exhibit distress in ways interpreted by the nursing or medical staff as some kind of illness, mental or physical, are given drugs officially. These tend to be prisoners who are a problem for the discipline staff, either because they are excessively violent or because they are suicidal. Excessive violence can conveniently be interpreted as paranoia, which makes drugging an acceptable way of handling the behaviour without having to examine anything in the prison system which is causing that behaviour. Suicides in prisons are administratively very tedious, so to avoid this risk drugs again become a way for personal issues on the part of the prisoner to be avoided. The rest of the prisoners have to rely on drugs being smuggled in occasionally by visitors as a gift or by prison staff.

A new phenomenon is identified in some prisons. There is an increasing number of young inmates so cut off from their feelings that they have no fear and no sense of compassion. They don't even have anger. The offences which brought them into prison tend to be extremely cold-blooded. They feel nothing about seriously mutilating someone for a trivial reason. When in prison they blackmail staff with threats to their family and children if not supplied with drugs. This apparent lack of feeling is, in every case, reinforced by the prison way of life.

Visits from the prisoner's family may be limited to one half-hour twice a month, but since that may involve a 400-mile round journey even such infrequent visits may not be possible. A day's journey with small children, or alternatively getting someone to care for them for the day, is not easy. If the prison is reasonably liberal, the family will meet in a large hall with perhaps another 100 people trying to talk to each other. Few prisons have play areas for children. In a less liberal setting, communication may only be possible through a wired pane of glass with an air inlet at the bottom of the pane. In order not to have to shout above the babble of noise around you have to spend the visit bent sideways so that your mouth and ear can alternately be pressed against the open mesh. It is degrading for both parties, and makes any serious or intimate conversation impossible.

When the expression of intimacy becomes impossible it has to be withdrawn. No one can go on indefinitely yearning for what is not available. In male prisons, while homosexual relationships exist they are less likely to be tolerated if they involve truly loving feelings. A 'hard' man may have a powerful homosexual aspect to his personality which can only be indulged in prison, but must be demonstrated as a power relationship, as the taking by force young, attractive prisoners. One such young man, who was forcibly raped three times in what is seen as one of the 'better' Scottish prisons, has just had it confirmed that he is HIV positive. His offence had been a minor fraud. It seems a heavy penalty.

When sexual tenderness is denied it is replaced by crudity and pornography. Cell walls are covered with fantasy women, always available, pouting and meaningless, two-dimensional figures available for any kind of degradation and brutality you want to inflict. The only kind of conversation about women permitted is crude and obscene but in a strange way this is a bridge between the prisoners and the staff who share these attitudes. The prison landing office is sometimes decorated (inside the cupboards) with unusually squalid pornography.

When prisoners are released and return home, the institutional defences cannot easily be given up. Yet it is impossible for an ordinary woman, perhaps with two or three young children, or by now middle-aged, to live up to the sexual fantasies built up within the containing cell. The reality is often a disappointment that cannot be discussed.

Another frequent difficulty is that over a period of years, constant masturbation, sometimes desperately engaged in for emotional comfort rather than sexual release, results in desensitization of the penis. The gentler grip of the female vagina, combined with a natural initial unwillingness to use prison pornographic imagery to achieve a climax, as in masturbation, may cause difficulty in reaching orgasm in the initial weeks or months after release. The man is forced back into masturbation, and may become convinced that he is permanently disabled. The woman may think she is no longer desired but neither may be able to discuss what is happening. Since for many men sexual capacity lies at the root of self-esteem, the chances are high that he will try to find another woman to reassure him. An encounter without real warmth, without loving feelings, but exciting in its strangeness, may help achieve his climax within the woman but will only reinforce the message of prison that life is simpler without feelings.

By creating and maintaining institutions that deny feelings of warmth and tenderness, by encouraging male competitive and aggressive styles of human encounter, prisons are killing off in prisoners those qualities most likely to help re-establish them in the community. (They also damage staff.) Simple social skills like apologizing are given no place because the most important thing is not to lose face. Yet I have seen innumerable jobs lost by ex-prisoners because one morning they came in late and when challenged couldn't give a simple explanation and express regret. Instead they bridled, told employers to stuff their jobs and walked out, cursing themselves. The same macho attitudes have an effect on their family life. The denial of tenderness cuts them off from communication with wives and children. At one time, no matter how they behaved, wives would accept it. That is no longer the case. She will leave, take the children with her and is often in no hurry to take on another man who cannot give her caring in return. So marriages break up, the man becomes rootless and homeless, and can either end up in prison again within a short time or else drift into destitution.

But many men succeed in a remarkable way in keeping their feelings alive in the most unlikely settings. They are loathe to admit it, but those few who have single cells will weep into their pillows at night. Men on the point of death by execution will call for their mothers. It is the capacity to feel, to reflect, to regret, to repent that distinguishes us from other creatures.

It is often said about notorious criminals that they have no feelings. This could be turned on its head. It may be that they have feelings stronger than law-abiding persons, which is why they have committed crimes. From infancy they may have wanted more than they were given, indeed, they may have needed more, more love, more attention, more education, more stimulation, more explanation about the nature of this world in which they found themselves. The institution should not deny these needs even more drastically but offer, at no matter how late a date, opportunities. For some it will be too late to fully recover more creative ways of asking the world to help them find what they need, rather than taking it brutally by theft, rape, or murder.

Most men and women would be better off for not going to prison at all. Since the penal institutions were built we have learned better ways of non-custodial punishment, such as fines, community service, compulsory weekend reporting and attendance. Other European countries use prison sentencing much less than Britain, and use it for shorter periods of time. For people who must be detained for the protection of the public because of the horrific nature of their crimes, we should be designing units which will genuinely help them to change to whatever extent is possible.

The women's movement in America, using its principles of non-violent confrontation, is developing some of the most hopeful ways of working with prisoners accused of rape and violence against women and children. They are concerned with the politics of male violence and the ways in which our patriarchal structures feed abuse of women and children. Going into the prisons, they meet and talk with the men responsible for these violent acts, demystifying the fantasies which have often been built up in isolation from women, and sharing feminine responses to feelings with the men. Simply locking up sex offenders is useless. We have to help them live in the world without causing harm to others.

There are some people so damaged that as yet we don't know how to help them live more creative lives. We know a little but not enough. What we do know is that it is impossible to write any human being off as permanently damaged. The human capacity to grow and develop from even the smallest seed of hope is a constant miracle. If we need any prisons – we certainly need far fewer than we have – it is around that miracle they should be designed. Instead of warehouses of pain and anger, they could offer experiences of community, responsibility and self-respect to both inmates and staff. Tears could be allowed onto the agenda of living.

If everyone in society outside had opportunities to be in touch with their feelings in work, education and creative living, fewer would end up in prison.

6

Tears and Grief

'I find myself weeping alone after the service.'

A church minister talking about his feeling that he shouldn't cry while doing his job of taking a funeral service even when he has known and loved the dead person.

A Zen monk travelling through a village, was told that the head of a family he knew had died. He sat down and wept. The villagers abused him, saying, 'You should help these people, not sit there weeping'. He answered, 'How can I help them if I am not able to weep?'

GRIEF AND COMMUNITY

Weeping alone is painful. Grief is most powerfully eased when it can be shared. We all find it difficult to walk alone in dark places, the forest, the deserted city streets, through the mysteries of death and our unanswered questions. We look for a hand to hold, a shoulder to weep on, another body to cling to – anything that will reassure us that we are not alone, abandoned and helpless in the face of forces we do not understand. Death is the most powerful of these forces.

In 1989 this was seen in Liverpool where the pain of the deaths of ninety-five football supporters was transformed into a collective sense of mutual caring and support. The Liverpool mourners were most fortunate than most. It is not a coincidence that their football supporters' song is 'You'll never walk alone'. That city, which has a long history of communal grief in the memories of Irish immigrants and desperate experiences of unemployment, knew, intuitively, how to behave. There was no attempt to hide the grief; it exploded, raw and naked. It was powered, as so much grieving is, not only by the act which had triggered it, but by community memories of other griefs. Ordinary life was halted to allow time for realization of the sorrow to penetrate the layers of defence that we all set up to blunt the terrible pain of loss. Rituals showed honour and reverence for the dead, not only the traditional laying of flowers, but the weaving into the fence of scarves and team colours which had intimate meaning for this occasion.

John Sweeney, writing in the *Observer* on the Sunday after the disaster, described 'the shrine' created at Liverpool's Anfield football stadium:

> Their faces tell the story. Some weep publicly; others walk high up into the stands and sob quietly. Still others are there to show their sympathy and respect, but also to see for themselves the spectacle of a city's mass grief.

And after a week, when the football ground had acted as a family home visited by friends from near and afar in what was a traditional wake, the flowers which had been laid were ritually burned. Then the more intimate funerals took place, the city began to return to normal and grieving continued at a more private level. The private level, while inevitably painful, had been given meaning and dignity by the first experience of community support.

We forget that early experiences of grief must have been communal, and still are in many societies. Where people have value as group members, our lives are not only our own or our immediate families'; in one sense they belong to the whole community, therefore each death is a loss to everyone. A public show of grief acknowledges that fact. The more significant the contribution of the dead person, the more powerfully the grief has to be shown, even if it means, as in some eastern countries, hiring women to act as professional mourners following the funeral procession, weeping and wailing. Until very recently in Ireland, keening, an indigenous form of wailing by women, was an important accompaniment of village funerals. Here we see traces of the power earlier societies attributed to women's tears as an aid to resurrection.

Since the earliest times religious rituals have surrounded the experiences of death, the disposal of the body of the deceased and formulas to aid grieving. In Judaism the bereaved person must be surrounded with friends and relatives for the first week and cared for. The Roman Catholic wake has served the same purposes. Protestantism brought more impersonal social sanctions for the bereaved, emphasizing behaviour rather than feelings, but continued to provide a strong framework within which grief could be experienced. In a secular society these practices have been weakened for many, leaving us bewildered about how to handle our grief.

BEREAVEMENT

We know an enormous amount about the processes of grieving for bereavement. We know only a little about how, in this more secular society, we should try to minimize the damage for people going through the grieving process. No one comes through it undamaged; the wound never wholly heals. Like a wound too, it has to be allowed to bleed, which is the function of our tears. It is an essential part of grieving that they be allowed to fall at some point, without restraint, if the healing process is to start.

We can hope, in time, again to give our love and commitment to some aspect of life. It may not be for a person's death or betrayal that we are grieving. We grieve also for the loss of an ideal or a belief, for changes in our body, a place we had to leave, an animal companion, even an illusion. Grieving can be for the loss of any person, idea or object giving meaning and significance to our lives. we may not even have loved them. It can be as important, sometimes even more important, to grieve for people whom we hated. For it is for ourselves and our own lost years that we grieve – years, happy and sad, that will not come again.

But bereavement is usually linked to the death of someone close, like our parents. Even if you are sixty or seventy years of age when that finally happens, your relationship with the world changes. You are now at the head of the personal queue filing toward the inevitability of death. None of us can conceive that we might die before our parents. They are a bulwark against that dark night: the candle that protected us in childhood. Now it is extinguished and we are alone in the dark. Your relationship with the world changes in another way. You are now a 'man' or a 'woman', rather than still being able to think of yourself as a child. We take into ourselves aspects of our parents that we may have denied previously. We may become more like them in our styles and habits; we may begin to look at our children as our parents looked at us; we may even assume that we will die at the age at which they died, and of the same disease or in the same way.

But reactions to parental death are not the same for everyone. We are more complicated. My first reaction to my mother's death was of relief. It took me a long time to admit that, but I gradually realized that many people were grateful to me for sharing the thought with them. It is more common than we realize. Some relief came from having the burden of exhaustion lifted. My mother's final illness had been long and painful for her and emotionally and physically demanding for me. But the whole of our relationship had been fraught with tension. Even when she was well, I had never been able to relax because I never knew from one day to the next how I was going to find her. Early in life she had managed to change roles with me, so that I felt responsible for her, rather than she for me. It was only long after her death that I realized how much anger lay under my acceptance of that responsibility and how much energy I had used holding that down.

At first I couldn't let myself grieve. On the afternoon of the funeral, not knowing what to do with myself, I went to a cinema which was practically empty. I sat in the front row of the balcony with tears rolling down my face and feeling nothing at all. My body was crying but my heart was empty. I couldn't let myself feel the pain until many years later and with the pain came anger.

No relationship is without conflict yet we rarely talk honestly about the faults of the person who has died. 'Do not speak ill of the dead', we are told, yet it is a great comfort to be with a friend who shares knowledge of how awful the dead person could sometimes be. Ministers, priests and those taking secular funerals need to find ways of giving a realistic rather than glamourized picture of the dead person. Some national newspapers have begun, in their obituary columns, to acknowledge that their subjects, no matter how distinguished, have been like the rest of us, part saint, part sinner.

Dr Cameron Macdonald, physician and therapist, talks about the three Rs that dominate our responses – Regret, Reproach and Relief. We regret the things we failed to do, we reproach ourselves for things we did do and feel relief that we have moved on. An inability to move through these feelings with some gentleness to ourselves can result in unresolved grief and even illness.

In this country we have lost many rituals that in the past supported us through the various stages of grief. We no longer wear mourning clothes for a fixed period of time, we don't refuse to go to parties for the first six months after the death of someone close to us, we don't take time immediately after the death for intensive grieving. As a result we don't give signals to our friends to sympathize in obvious ways. On the contrary we openly challenge the old rituals. We turn up to funerals in everyday clothes, we refuse to let people send flowers so there is no opportunity for a communal expression of feeling, we are reluctant to take more than one day off work on the grounds that we're better getting on with life as if weeping and mourning had no part in real life. Worse, we give no signals to *ourselves* that we need time to grieve. We abandon the support of formal steps that move us out of that grief back into loving life.

The funeral ritual is particularly important in providing an end point. Even in the Lockerbie disaster, where a plane exploded in mid-air, and many bodies could only be pieced together in fragments, relatives came from the other side of the world searching for something, anything that gave a focus to their grief and over which they could weep. Terrible problems arise for survivors of death at sea or explosions where not even fragments are left. One group who also suffer deeply are secret, adulterous lovers where one partner is killed and the survivor is unable to see the body or go to the funeral. Sometimes they are unable to tell any other human being of their loss.

The relatives of those who commit suicide face great conflicts. They are expected by friends and neighbours to follow the normal passages of grieving, yet often they are consumed with anger. It is as if the dead person had killed themselves in order to get away and as a punishment. The act of suicide among younger people is indeed often an act of anger against those with whom they live, and who have failed to solve their problems. Some people seem to stage their suicides in ways which punish the survivor. I knew one family where the husband hung himself facing the front door so that his body would be the first thing his wife would see as she came in. The mixture of anger and guilt which overwhelmed his widow made it impossible for her to grieve and weep for the loss of the good things shared in the early days of their marriage.

For the children of suicides there is an equal if not greater burden to bear. At some level every child is aware of being their parent's future and by this act, the parent is rejecting what they offer. They have turned aside from pride and pleasure in their child, they have withdrawn any investment in their future, they have foregone the potential joy of grandchildren. How can a child or young person immediately grieve for someone who denies their existence in that way? There are many layers of hurt to peel off before they can see their parent as a human being seeking a way out of a private torment.

One owes respect to the living; but to the dead one owes nothing but the truth.

                                                                Voltaire

It is not surprising that, in these jungles of feeling, other people's responses to our grieving is awkward and embarrassed. Other people's grief stirs our own unshed tears. Because there are no rituals to handle this confusion of feeling, friends may avoid us, even by crossing to the other side of the street. Part of this comes from a superstitious but unacknowledged sense that grief is contagious and unlucky. The bereaved are dimly aware of these feelings, and are equally embarrassed about displaying tears. They can avoid their friends and, when they see them, hide signs of distress, not wanting to be a 'nuisance'. A nameless sense of guilt accompanies some bereaved, as if they are mysteriously to blame.

Women traditionally show their grief more than men. This makes it more likely that they will be avoided. This can include a reluctance to ask them to visit, or to come for a meal and even the fear, felt by some women, that a grieving woman may attract their own husbands. Grieving men are easier to deal with. It is acceptable to ask them over for a meal, they are not expected to be able to manage without a caring woman. They arouse protectiveness in women and are not seen as a threat by other men. The fact that they show little grief does not mean they are unmoved, but they may have been less inclined than are many women to see their relationship with their partner as the fulcrum of their lives.

One profession which sees more of the bereaved than the rest of us are undertakers. Perhaps twenty times a week each one has to confront a dead body; they have to meet, talk with and help relatives and friends cope with the practical arrangements posed by the death. No matter what the feelings of the bereaved, the body has to be got out of the way, buried or burned, and much of the richest information from earlier societies comes from the importance accorded to that act. All other creatures on the planet leave the dead bodies of their own kind to rot in the open air. Only humans have devised complicated rituals which convey mystery and respect, along with mourning and tears.

The code of practice of the Association of Funeral Directors describes every step of their procedures for dealing with a dead body but constantly emphasizes the need to behave with respect, the need to act 'as if the next-of-kin were standing at their elbow, or act as they would if the deceased were a member of their own family'. We all recognize how important these conventions are. For those of us who, after the Second World War, sat riveted to cinema screens up and down the country as we watched the opening up of the concentration camps, watched the piled-up heaps of dead bodies, our whole perception of civilized behaviour was outraged. It was a fundamental assault on our sensibility and aroused a horror almost too deep for tears.

But the equally necessary professional detachment of undertakers gives them a valuable view of human reactions. They see the range of responses from deep and bitter grief to awkward attempts to simulate grief where it no longer has relevance for the relationship. They identify people who need counselling help and may refer them to the priest or minister; they recognize their own rituals as important aids to grieving.

Denial and anger – the cycle of despair

The first reaction to the death of someone important to us is usually disbelief, just as to news of our own impending death. The human psyche finds the idea of its own destruction intolerable and another's death can be a threat to our fantasies of immortality. This comes even when death has been expected for some time, but is even more dramatic when the death is sudden. Powerful public examples of this were seen in photographs taken after the death of the American president J.F. Kennedy who had become a great folk hero to the American people. His death was seen on television by millions of people, but for days afterwards they were caught by the cameras staring unbelievingly into space. They couldn't believe what had happened. We saw the same unbelieving stares on the faces of the Americans who watched the 'Challenger' failure.

We go into a state of shock to protect us from the knowledge. A kind of numbness acts as a shell against not only death itself, but against all the implications of loss that go with it. Occasionally the shell cracks, awareness creeps in and normally tears and bitter weeping come. When the pain becomes intolerable, the numbness and disbelief take over again to protect us. The cycle keeps repeating. At this stage you are normally expected to experience grief when the main feeling is shock. Real grief comes later: only then are you ready to share your deep suffering. People in contact with the bereaved (and the bereaved themselves) find this time-lag disconcerting. The grief can be displaced and a man unable to cry at his father's funeral may find himself crying for days three months later when his spaniel dies.

But the story is unfinished. Another normal step in the process of grieving, one which often follows closely on numbness, is anger, often just free-floating anger without specific focus and likely to last until around the anniversary of the death which caused it. This is often the feeling the bereaved find most difficult to acknowledge, their anger against the dead person for abandoning them to face the world alone. Rationality is irrelevant. Under our sophistication we are simple souls. When we were small our loved parents would sometimes leave us when we didn't want them to go. We were bereft. We didn't understand the good reasons why they couldn't be with us. All we knew was that they were not there when we needed them, and we blamed them. Why should we not? Old habits die hard. Scratch any of us and you will find a small child. The loss of anyone close and deeply loved rouses the same feelings of anger.

In the confusion of this anger both men and women may turn to a friend or even a stranger for a sexual encounter, often to the scandal of friends and neighbours. Few people try to understand how, if the bereaved truly loved their partner, they can behave in this 'shameless' way. Yet it is because they loved their partner so deeply that they are driven to seek ways of easing their pain and fear. One middle-aged woman whose husband died suddenly of a heart attack reacted with a storm of sexual behaviour with a succession of younger men. Her family was scandalized because she made no effort to hide what she was doing. She was amazed by her own behaviour and between episodes was bitterly ashamed of what was happening to her. For about fifteen months after her husband's death she felt driven into these encounters.

She came out of the need quite suddenly one afternoon when, after sex, her partner held her tenderly, which none of the others had done. She began to cry, not the angry, resentful tears she'd cried after her husband's death, but like a small child seeking comfort. Fortunately the man was able to let her weep and talk about the pain. After this experience she was celibate for about three years. Later she married a man of about her own age, in many ways very like her former husband. She can now talk about her anger at being suddenly deserted, and see that her behaviour was a shouted defiance of the world she no longer felt able to trust.

Anger against the person who has died can be experienced as dangerous and may not be tolerated by the bereaved, so other outlets for our anger and sense of loss have to be found. It is not always realized that the pain of loss is experienced physically as well as mentally. Many people can point to the part of their bodies where the pain is felt. In order to ease it many diversions are tried. Some women attack their own bodies, scratching and tearing at their skin until the blood runs. They tug at their hair, pulling it out at the roots, roll around the floor and bang their heads against the wall. The physical pain brings a temporary sense of relief. All these activities are also seen in the behaviour of children grossly neglected and deprived of affection and attention.

Other people turn their anger outwards. Doctors and hospitals are a good target, 'they should be made to pay'; the man driving the other car 'should go to prison for life'; the murderer should be hung. After the Sheffield football disaster, within a week we heard accusations against the police, against the clubs, against the fans themselves who were accused of being drunk and causing trouble. In seeking revenge, we seek to rid ourselves of pain. We seek to rid ourselves of the awful thought that we might have some responsibility for what has happened. The thought of our own guilt threatens our very existence. Our lives are miserable as we remember times when we might have been kinder, we might have been more loving, less impatient. We wake up during the night with desperate thoughts of what horrible people we are and how if others knew what we were really like they would never want to see us again.

Some people get stuck at this point. They move backward and forward between denial and anger and depression, unable to break out of the circle of despair by acceptance of what has happened. They are unable to enter into a total experience of mourning where they acknowledge loss and pain without needing to deny it or blame anyone. Only when that has been fully experienced can the bereaved person take what had been the good parts of the lost relationship and find a new relationship into which those positive feelings can be renewed.

We all know widowers and widows who have failed to recover from loss, whose family or friends can find no way of breaking into their misery and sadly, but inevitably, become tired of trying. Visiting them becomes a draining experience which is avoided. It is often partners who have been most able to express their feelings, who are more likely to find new partners after a bereavement by investing feeling in a new relationship.

The dark night of the soul

We have to go through the 'dark night of the soul', and that involves using both our minds and our bodies. We have this remarkable gift of tears, which will in time ease both our physical and emotional pain. One woman described how she had gone back to work after the death of her husband, determined to be brave. She kept maniacally busy so as not to feel sorrow and set herself the goal of working so hard that at night she fell into bed exhausted. She would wake in the night hearing sobs, then realize they were hers and immediately stop. After some weeks, instead of taking a sleeping pill she decided to lie awake and feel what her body was telling her. She began to think of her husband and how much she missed having the comfort of his body in bed. She began to cry, deep powerful gut-wrenching sobs, more painful than anything she had ever known. They went on for three hours before she fell asleep, exhausted but more relaxed than since her husband died. She said later that it was the same kind of relaxation the body feels after a really satisfying orgasm, every muscle relaxed and a marvellous sense of peace. She stayed off work that morning and for the rest of the week. She stayed at home, weeping intermittently but never again with the same passion and desperation of that first outburst. She went over the whole experience of first meeting her husband, their courtship and marriage and life together. She talked to friends, not only about the happy times they'd had together but the inevitable disappointments. She faced her anger at being abandoned at an earlier age than anyone would have expected, and talked about loneliness. Hour after hour, the thoughts she had been pushing back came pouring out.

Weak but feeling, as she put it, 'lighter', she returned to work. She was able to warn her manager that for a while she might be a bit slower and occasionally a bit tearful. Her colleagues were relieved that the tense, frantic performance given since her husband's death had stopped. They hadn't known how to get through to her, and were happy to give support.

Each of us brings to grieving everything else that has happened in our lives. Somewhere in our heads we carry every grief experienced, and in any new loss, each comes to life again. We are likely to repeat previous styles to get us through the pain, but a point can be reached where the old ways no longer work. Our capacity to deny or block out the pain can wear thin. Sometimes our bodies and minds seek excuses to experience griefs that we may have put aside or denied because we couldn't face them at the time. Ruth Rendell in her novel *The Face of Trespass*, describes how a man burns his hand on an iron:

> When he looked at his hand there was a bright red weal across the palm . . . he held his hand under the cold tap. The shock was so great that it brought tears to his eyes, and when he'd turned off the tap and dried his hand, the tears didn't stop. He began to cry in earnest, abandoning himself to a storm of weeping, sobbing against his folded arms. He knew he wasn't crying because he'd burnt his hand, though that had caused the tears. Full release had never come to him before, the release of all that pent-up pain. He was crying now . . . for loneliness and squalor and waste.

A child's right to grieve

He was also crying as a child cries when hurt, with the whole of itself. If, as children, we were given healing opportunities to grieve for a range of losses, whether it was falling and losing our precariously-achieved sense of balance, the death of a cat, the breaking of a doll or having to move house, we will have learned skills which will stand us in good stead later. Many children are not helped. 'Don't be silly', 'don't make such a fuss', are the messages from parents who don't appreciate the intensity of children's grief.

When parents exclude children from their own grief it can make the child feel that the awful event that has taken place is a punishment for which they are in part responsible. The parent's intention is often to protect so they hide tears and sorrowing putting on a ghastly pretence of cheerfulness. A child who has lost its father either by death or divorce is not helped by a mother who denies her own sadness. One young woman whose husband was killed in an air crash described how all her friends had said she mustn't cry in front of her six-year-old daughter. They said she must stay cheerful for the child's sake. So she saved her tears until she was in bed.

After about two years she met a man whom she loved and agreed to marry although worried that her daugher had stayed very withdrawn from him. When she told her of the plan to marry the child's feelings came out. She said, 'You're glad Daddy died, aren't you!' She had assumed that because mother hadn't wept or shown grief that her father hadn't been loved by anyone but herself and her father's parents, who wept copiously. Ironically the mother had been supporting them in their grief, while hiding her own. Her daughter's attack made her break down and weep, and after they'd cried together they talked about the misunderstandings. The mother postponed her second marriage for six months to give time to sort out the new relationships. The three of them were able to use some sessions of family therapy to acknowledge the need to grieve for the past as well as to prepare for the future.

For a parent to hide sorrow or even anger denies the child's right to have their own feelings. Our grief is our own and no one has the right to take it away. It always reclaims us. Unresolved mourning has the capacity to erupt as an overwhelming crisis when a further bereavement is faced, not only of a death, but also of a loss to one's life-purpose, like redundancy or retirement.

GRIEVING FOR OURSELVES

One man, trying to find his own tears, turned to looking at why he never cried for his father. His early experiences included savage beatings, carried on until his teens. These had been given, he was told, 'in order to teach you respect'. He left home as early as possible, did well in his career and visited his parents as seldom as possible. When his father died he felt nothing and had done nothing more than take a day off for the funeral. He couldn't bear to hear his mother mourn for her loss so continued to visit infrequently, leaving the main responsibility to his sister, who genuinely mourned her father. It was the birth of his own son that confronted him with questions. He wanted to do a better job than his father had done with him. With help, he explored his feelings and to his horror found himself crying, not for his father, but for himself. He was grieving for his own pain and sense of loss at not having a father whom he could love. Until he worked through that he was unable to see his father as a human being. On a visit to his mother he began to ask her what his father's life had been like. His father had been savagely beaten himself as a child, and had gone through life feeling a failure. He had tried to beat his son into giving him the respect he was unable to feel for himself. The tears that came with this knowledge were now true tears of grieving for his father's death, and the knowledge that they would never communicate with each other. He remembered not only his father's harshness, but that he had worked hard and struggled to give both children a good education, holidays abroad and a comfortable home, all things he'd never had himself.

There is a sense in which all grieving is for ourselves, so whether or not we loved the lost one can be irrelevant: all that matters is that they played an important part in our lives. When they go they take part of us with them. We may have shared experiences of love, anger or fear. They may have been colleagues, school friends or bowls partners with whom we shared moments of laughter, persecution or triumph. It is for ourselves and our lost youth we weep. We may need to grieve when we leave places where we have been happy and even places where we have been unhappy, like prisons or boarding schools. It can be painful to leave the house in which we were born or the house in which our children were born. I know one woman who can't bear to throw away the bed in which her children were born! The hardest loss for many is to move ultimately from their own home to a home for the elderly, a move which they recognize may well be the last one they will ever make, and which forces them to confront their own death.

He that conceals his grief finds no remedy for it.

Turkish proverb.

Grief over ageing

A major source of distress for both men and women is the process
of ageing. Jung said that we cannot live the afternoon of life
according to the programme of life's morning. What in the morning was true will in the evening become a lie. Our bodies begin to
give us messages we would be wise to accept. Vast industries grow
up to reinforce our fear and denial, help us stay unwrinkled,
maintain our hair colour, postpone sagging muscles. We are
spurred on by advertising images that fun is for the young and fit.
To be old is to be wrinkled and crabbit and heading for Parkinson's
or Altzheimer's disease. We are told that the elderly are living too
long, will cost the country too much money and there will be no
services enabling them to live with dignity. But no matter what
cosmetics we use, what exercises we do, the decay of our bodies
moves inexorably forward.

Middle age, when most messages of what faces us begin to
appear, is a gift time. It is a time when we can take a deep breath,
assess where we are and make a start on our anticipatory mourning for our fate. We must neither deny what is going to happen to
us, nor fall into a depression without hope. Mourning and depression are not the same thing. Mourning is a much more conscious
process where we can focus on a loss, either which we have
experienced or which we are going to experience. Depression
normally catches us unawares. Mourning is something we can
choose to do. Depression is something we allow to happen if we
choose not to mourn.

PREPARING FOR GRIEF

The value of anticipatory mourning has been proved in hospital
work, where patients who know in advance that they are going to
have an operation which entails the loss of a breast, a testicle or a
limb have an opportunity to talk before the operation about their
fears and anxieties. They are encouraged to do 'worry work', to ask
questions about what is going to happen, to weep if they feel like
it, to ask for and get reassurance that the future will be all right;
different but all right. Reults show that these patients recover at a
much faster rate, that they are more optimistic, less 'self-pitying'
and demand less time and attention from nursing staff than those

who did not have the opportunity for anticipatory mourning.

This applies also to those waiting for the death of someone close. If they totally deny what is going to happen, the ultimate grieving is much, much harder. The waiting time can be used to say goodbye to different aspects of the life we had with the person who is dying. A friend of mine married late and had seven extraordinarily happy years before her husband fell at her feet one day, struck down by a cerebral haemorrhage. It took him two weeks to die and for the second of those we spoke together every night by telephone, often for more than an hour. We talked about the possibility of his death, we talked about the possibility of him being permanently brain damaged, we talked about the happiness they had enjoyed together and how important it had been to both of them to find each other. When the time came for the machine which had been keeping her husband alive to be turned off, my friend faced the reality of his condition and let him go. She was able to let him go as he was now because she had clarified and confirmed what he had been to her. She grieved deeply for him but without bitterness; at one level she is still grieving years later but it is not a destructive grieving. She has continued to grow and has chosen to develop those qualities which her husband most loved in her, her resoluteness, her courage, and her ability to stay open to the world.

UNEXPECTED DISASTER

Those who can fully grieve over an unexpected disaster, like the sudden loss of a limb or blindness, will be in a far better state to make the best use of the faculties left. The experience of rehabilitation centres is that people who come to them having been conscientiously cheerful since the day of their loss, who have never wept or allowed themselves to enter fully into the pain of their loss, find it much more difficult to acquire new skills. It's as if the denial of the pain inhibits their capacity to learn. To put all their energy into learning skills which would enable them to cope with their disability would mean admitting that they are disabled. Bringing that thought into consciousness means going through the classical stages of acknowledging the anger and the pain before finding acceptance. Only with acceptance will they find emotional freedom and energy.

Health professionals, particularly doctors, find particular difficulty in coping with a disabling illness in adult life. They feel they ought to be immune and, in their health, superior to lay people. The denial can be so strong that faced, for example, with diabetes, they fail to take their diet or their insulin. Only a dramatic confrontation with the reality of their condition will make them take their illness seriously.

There are many people who collude with their partner, or loved one, or friend's denial of loss or suffering because they cannot face the other person's pain and tears. It is easier to go along with the false cheerfulness. It is often left to professional counsellors like social workers and therapists to help the disabled person and their family cope with reality. The processes of denial and anger have to be given their place before proper grieving can begin.

The birth of a damaged or handicapped child can be unbelievably painful. It means the loss of hopes and plans which have been building up in the parents during the months of pregnancy. The professionals involved, the doctors and nurses, can find it deeply disturbing to tell the patients what they have to face. The most helpful sources of support are more likely to be the parents of other children who have experienced the same trauma. They understand, because they have been there themselves. They know the range of conflicting feelings which need to be worked through before tears of anger can become the healing tears of grief. Those who cannot allow themselves to experience the pain and the guilt that goes with it cannot move through to acceptance and therefore some more creative response. Unless parents fully accept the child, the burden of pain and failure will be passed on.

A very powerful account, *And I Don't Want To Live This Life*, was written by the mother of a girl who, from infancy, had behaved in what seemed abnormal ways. At the age of twenty, after a life of violent and addictive behaviour, the girl, Nancy, was murdered. What is remarkable about this story is how the mother finally found peace and came to terms with her daughter's life as well as her death. During the twenty years of worry and despair she had not cried. She said there was never time. One day after her daughter's death, she was driving to see a new house to which the family planned to move.

Suddenly I felt something hot on my hands.

I looked down. My hands were drenched with tears. I looked

at myself in the rearview mirror. Tears were rolling down my cheeks. Twenty years' worth. They were finally pouring out on their own. I couldn't stop them. My vision began to blur. I was afraid I'd lose control of the car. I pulled over to the emergency lane, barely able to see the other cars on the road. When I'd come to a safe stop and turned off the motor, I broke down and sobbed. I sobbed and sobbed uncontrollably. I cried a torrent of tears. Tears of frustration, anger, pain and grief.

I cried for my baby.

The crying continued after that, and continues, but now with other parents who face the same kinds of problems. Deborah Spungen set up a support organization for the parents of murdered children. In doing this she demonstrated the way in which, having once made contact with one's feelings, it becomes possible to convert pain into creative action. Once we have made contact with pain we can use the energy it holds. I could fill pages and pages with lists of self-help groups that have grown out of this discovered energy. In Britain alone there are 25,000 concerned with health issues of one kind or another, not only physical but mental illness as well.

Perhaps we need to develop groups for 'failures', for children born with or who develop conditions which make them unable to fit labels of normality. They are acutely conscious of having failed parental expectations. They hide this from their parents so as not to add to their pain, but need someone with whom they can share unacceptable feelings. We concentrate so much on parental disappointment that we forget the other face of the coin. Children with Down's syndrome, children with learning difficulties or with a physical handicap, no matter how loved, are acutely aware of how they are seen by the world.

LOSING A COUNTRY: LOSING A JOB

One of the most poignant losses any human being faces is having to leave one's home and sometimes even one's country because of war, racism, famine or simply the drive to get decent economic opportunities. America was built on this kind of distress and its culture was enriched by literature and songs full of nostalgia, yearning and grief. Every immigrant family carries this sense of pain somewhere in its psyche, but often it is left to the women to hold the sense of pain and loss while the husbands and children find their way in the new world. To-day we can see Pakistani or Bengali women, walking in their traditional clothes, barely able to understand the language of the country in which they are living, acting as the repository for the pain and grief of the whole family. In some way we do not fully understand, if one member of the family can do this it releases the energy of the others. But someone has to be willing to carry the burden. It is a heavy one, and traditionally left for women.

What we know less about is the pain of the families left behind in the 'Old Country' who have to watch the young people leave. In Scotland and Ireland whole communities were bereft. The arrival of a letter from a son or daughter was an event in which tears of relief were mixed with tears of sorrow, and the news was shared with the whole community. In Ireland the departure of the emigrant was ritualized with a procession to the boat or the railway station. They called it 'a living wake'.

For many men the most important grieving they do is over the loss of their work when made redundant or on retirement. Most men are taught to seek in their working lives the sense of purpose, of meaning and of self-respect that women seek in personal relationships. A job gives structure and a reason for getting up in the morning: it gives human contact with colleagues, it gives 'busyness'. It gives them an answer to that most terrible question, 'And what do you do?' Men have great difficulty, because of their conditioning, to see 'being' as important. For most, 'doing' is everything.

So when the job goes they feel their soul has gone with it. Yet they are not supposed to grieve. They are supposed to be cheerful and rejoice, when they want to weep with terror and self-pity. They have no helpful rituals. Their farewell party is a sham and a mockery, a pretence that a great future awaits them instead of the fear that the next great event in their lives may be their death. And everyone joins in this charade with talk of them now having time to do all the things they have always wanted to do. 'Drop in when you're passing', they say, but nothing but humiliation faces those who do, and see someone else at the desk that was once their's and find everyone too busy to chat. 'We'll lunch when you're in town', they say – and no-one believes it. And indeed for the first few weeks there is a manic response of getting up at the usual time and finding things to do, but which gradually subsides into grief and depression.

There are lucky people who have jobs which can continue long past retirement age; they will live longer as a result. Others prepare themselves through pre-retirement planning to find ways of giving continuing service to the community. There are also people of a naturally equable temperament who intuitively understand the need for preparatory mourning and adjust their lives accordingly. But without another job, a hobby or some activity that gives meaning to their lives there is danger. Recent German statistics show that 30 per cent of retired people who have nothing that interests them, die within a year of retirement, regardless of the age at which they retired.

It is a very different matter for younger people made redundant without warning. For them the whole range of feelings of shock, disbelief and anger come into play. Unless they are given opportunities to express their grief in appropriate ways which can include weeping for loss, they will never be able to acquire the creative energy necessary to find a new job. In close communities like mines, the workers have been able to express both grief and anger openly. It is in the newer manufacturing industries that factories have been closed and the workers have walked away, numbed and despairing.

THE GRIEF OF DISILLUSION

These are just some of the losses we may experience in life. Some, like our own ageing or the death of friends or loved ones, are inevitable for all of us who live long enough. But there are other less obvious losses that happen to some people for which the grieving and mourning patterns are just as relevant. Many people who were young in the thirties of this century had a love affair with Communism. The Russian revolution had swept away the most cruel and backward government in Europe and become a symbol of hope for many people, a symbol that ideas of freedom and justice could overcome tyranny. What was not understood was that when you sweep away a feudal society, you do not overnight change the institutions or the casts of thought that have been built up over centuries. Nor in those pre-Holocaust years had innocent belief in human progress been lost. So with the gradual release of information about Stalinism and the terrible losses of life in the labour camps, a whole generation of political activists lost their faith, not only in Russia, but in the hope that human beings can radically alter their society in ways that make it more equal and more just.

There were some who denied their loss and held on to formulas of belief but by far the largest numbers of devotees simply withdrew from political activity into a position of depression. They were unable to confront their pain and anger. There were a few people who allowed themselves to feel the pain of loss, the pain of betrayal, when they began to understand what had really been happening in the Soviet Union. I knew men and women who wept bitter tears as they confronted how they had given their love, their time, their heart's energy to a cause which they now saw as false. These were the people who used that experience to free themselves from intellectual slavery to any party, but who did not lose the innocence of faith in the human capacity to change the world for the better.

The changes which took place in Eastern Europe during 1989 and 1990 pose some of the same problems. There are terrible stories of what happened, how corruption spread and how power was abused. Except for a few people in each country who tried to keep protest alive, everyone else shares responsibility. The citizens of these countries have somehow to find forgiveness for each other and for themselves as part of the process of grieving and healing. In many areas of our lives we have to face what T.S. Eliot described as,

> . . . *the rending pain of re-enactment*
> *Of all that you have done, and been; the shame*
> *Of motives late revealed, and the awareness*
> *Of things ill done and done to others' harm*
> *Which once you took for exercise of virtue.*

Closer to home is the trauma faced by social workers over the last ten years. This profession, which most members had come to brimming with conviction that they had found a way of linking their idealism to an honourable way of earning a living, has been devastated by continuous attack from the media. They have felt misunderstood and scapegoated, quite unprepared for the political and social dilemmas in which they were caught. Many have moved from saying proudly they were social workers to saying it with embarrassment.

Grieving for the lost image of ourselves as helpful and useful people can be an important factor in avoiding depression or cynicism and recovering our self-respect. Too often we have let ourselves be locked into a 'graven image' of ourselves, perhaps by parents and teachers. Only by shedding that can we become humble. Grief and tears are not to be seen as special experiences, only to be used at great and solemn moments. They can be woven into the fabric of everyday life, the human experiences of trying and failing. They give us courage to try again and to succeed.

GRIEVING AND LETTING GO

But a primary condition is that we have to let go of those aspects of our past that are no longer helpful or relevant. The growth of every living creature or plant on the planet is dependent on the casting-off of parts that have served their purpose. If they were held on to the animal or plant would die. The cells of our skin are constantly dying and being replaced, the old ones have to be sloughed off to make space for the new. Similar changes are constantly taking place in other parts of our bodies. In the plant world new growth cannot take place until the old has died and dropped away. The seasons of the year reflect the cycle of life.

Within the human spirit the same processes are present. The small child has to pay a price for every step she makes to independence. To feed oneself means giving up the marvellous comfort of being fed, to walk alone means giving up the pleasant passivity of being carried. And so it goes on through life; always a struggle between wanting to hold on to what we have at the same time as we are reaching out for new joys and satisfactions; always the dilemma of making choices, of greedily wanting everything, of resenting having to let anything go. Every step forward requires of us the abandonment of the past.

If we try to hold on to everything we end up with nothing. The man or woman whose marriage is a mess, who seeks a more loving relationship with a succession of lovers, but who can never bring themselves either to leave or be honest with their partner, is caught in a cycle of small deaths with no hope of life. Others who hold on either to resentments of the past or else to romanticised versions of past events are equally unable to grow. What is sad is that caught in this way, they are unable to see or use the opportunities for life-fulfilling experiences spread out before them. The ability to let go of parts of our past, of parts of ourselves, of fantasies, of dreams that are no longer relevant, of pain that has long since served its purpose, is an essential part of our capacity to grieve and to recreate ourselves. It is for the loss of these things that we weep and it is in the weeping that we clear the path for renewal of our hope and trust in life itself, rather than in individual and fragile dreams.

Every change in our lives brings with it griefs, even changes for the better. For that reason, conservatives who reject the idea of change, who cling to past ideas and ideologies, while we may not agree with them, are entitled to be understood and their reluctance to face the pain of change respected. But sometimes that reluctance means that others are immured in their pain. All social progress has caused pain to some but liberated others. Those of us who wish to push forward must acknowledge the pain it may cause and help those affected to grieve, and then to let go of values and ideas which may no longer be relevant. But we must also, where possible, build into plans for the future those values that are worth preserving.

7

Tears and Religion

Jesus wept.

John, 11:35

One autumn day, while working in the library, I found a book which described weeping rituals in ancient Canaan. At the end of each summer, when the grass turned brown and the growing cycle had ended, groups of women came together in the fields for a ceremony of weeping. It was thought that the god of fertility had died and only their tears could bring him back. In this way fertility would be renewed and another season begun. It was as if the energy of their tears revived him. At a certain point in the ceremony the rhythm of the weeping began to change and the tears were replaced by laughter and sometimes a kind of ecstatic, even erotic frenzy.

I was moved by the account, seeing resemblances between the experience of these women, dead many thousands of years before, and women alive now who weep over men whose love they think is dead but try to revive with their tears. Sometimes such weeping is transformed into an erotic frenzy which may or may not refertilize powerful feelings between them.

On the following day, I went to Greenham Common where women were arriving from all over Europe to take part in a demonstration against the nuclear weapons housed there. It was a dull, grey day as if the sky was mourning with us. At one of the gates in the fence which circled the base, a religious service was held which attracted both Christians and non-Christians. A cloth was spread on the ground, candles placed in jam jars on the corners, a loaf in the middle. Then to the tune of 'By the waters of Babylon I sat down and wept', we sang another version of the words. The soldiers and police guarding the gate heard, 'By the wires of Greenham, we sit down and weep, weep for this our land'. As the women's voices soared and broke into part-singing so that the phrase 'We sit down and weep' rang round and round the group, the hair prickled on the back of my neck. A ball of green wool was passed around and we used it to bind ourselves together as the singing continued. Next, long white streamers tied into an intricate pattern in the centre were handed to various women standing in the circle. Then the priestess – for that is what she was – began to weave a web while talking about her reasons for being at Greenham. She passed the streamer to another woman who did the same and each woman who received it made a statement of her sorrow, culminating with a young woman who spoke, with tears running down her face, of her fears for her children. By the time she had finished, most of us were openly weeping with her, and the web was half finished.

Then subtly the tone began to change. Courage and hope emerged and by the time the web was finished, the bread broken and shared, people were smiling and charged with energy. What to do with the beautiful web we had made? Still tied together with the strands of wool we moved towards the fence intending to drape it on the wire. Then the movement shifted and we veered to the gate. It was like being part of an uncertain creative organism. Then with a sudden ecstatic rush, we all resolved at once that it should be put up across the gate and the military must accept responsibility for destroying it.

As I disentangled myself from the green wool, I had been linked not only to these women beside me, but to those in Canaan and all the other women through the centuries who have wept over the death of the gods of life, of love, and of hope, whom they tried to revive with their tears.

When the Israelite desert tribes entered Canaan, they found a land not only flowing with milk and honey, but full of weeping and laughter in its religious rituals, quite different from anything they had known. They also entered a world of very different beliefs from their own. All the food available to animals and man was thought to be due to the rain which fell from the heavens, the arrival of which was dependent on the will of the god Ba'al. Each year Ba'al died at the end of the harvest, was revived, then ascended to his throne and opened a cleft in the clouds so that the rain could fall. It was the Lord Ba'al's love for the virgin Anat that brought him back from the dead, in response to her tears. All animal and human fertility depended on this ritual being acted out. The whole population joined in the autumn festival. Sacrifices were offered while the women noisily wailed and wept. Ba'al was thought to have descended into the earth and the sacrifices and energy invigorated him and brought about his resurrection. But the rejoicing and the laughter which followed the tears were of equal importance, because they powered the erotic joy that was as important as the water falling from the sky.

From the resurrection of Ba'al, to the resurrection of Christ, the rituals have changed; even the meaning given to the weeping has changed; but the power of tears remains. They became an essential part of the practices of the Israelite tribes who penetrated to the northern parts of Canaan and integrated with local people. The Old Testament identifies holy places which were probably early cultic weeping places. One was the grave of Rachel, where 'Lamentation is heard in Ra-mah and bitter weeping'. Almost certainly before Rachel an ancient goddess shed tears there bewailing her lover and, as Anat did for Ba'al, she 'continued sating herself with weeping, To drink tears like wine'.

The other side of the weeping was the cultic ecstasy and the wild erotically-charged energy which followed it. The goddess was recognized as a partner in fertility. These responses began to permeate Israelite life: and the prophet Jeremiah preached against the cults and idolatry. Women were most resistant to his strictures, claiming that when they served the goddess, they were never short of food. The prophets won. A transformation began which to this day influences our use of tears and lamentation. The ancient rituals which linked them to fertility and the renewal of life were abandoned. Yahweh, the God of Israel, eliminated Ba'al by becoming the lord of all growth and fertility. He needed no help from men and women, and needed no partner. In this move power was taken away from the people as participants in the ritual and invested totally in the god. The only part left was the male role of sacrifice; the generative power of women's tears was excluded. Weeping became a self-humiliation, an acknowledgement of one's unworthiness before the god, used only to appeal to Yahweh in the hope of influencing His decisions.

From the end of the period of the Kings, public penitential festivals were a frequent necessity. When there were droughts, crop failure or disease, disgrace or defeat in war, the people were summoned to participate in public weeping and rituals of mourning. A time for weeping and lamentation was fixed and announced, when 'all the country wept with a loud voice'. At the individual level man, because women's role in ritual was now eliminated, had to appear before God to confess his sins. Shame, repentance and weeping served this confession. Weeping had now become linked with penance and fasting.

Christianity continued the penitential tradition and the 'grace of tears' was considered one of the chief gifts offered to the penitent. Their power was still recognized. St Bernard tells us that 'the tears of the humble can penetrate to heaven and conquer the unconquerable'. The conclusion drawn in the *Malleus Maleficarum*, the handbook on witchcraft written in 1486 by two Dominican friars, was that this made tears displeasing to the Devil, and he made it impossible for witches to cry so that they would never find repentance.

This theory became the basis for the examination and torture of those suspected of witchcraft. The judge is advised that:

> If he wishes to find out whether she is endowed with a witch's power of preserving silence, let him take note whether she is able to shed tears when standing in his presence or when being tortured. For we are taught both by the words of worthy men of old and by our experience that this is a most certain sign, and it has been found that even if she be urged and exhorted by solemn conjurations to shed tears, if she be a witch she will not be able to weep: although she will assume a tearful aspect and smear her cheeks and eyes with spittle to make it appear that she is weeping; wherefore she must be closely watched by the attendants.

In passing sentence the judge was advised to place his hand on the head of the accused and say,

> I conjure you by the bitter tears shed on the Cross by our Saviour the Lord JESUS Christ for the salvation of the world, and by the burning tears poured in the evening hour over His wounds by the most glorious Virgin MARY, His Mother, and by all the tears which have been shed here in this world by the Saints and Elect of God from whose eyes He has now wiped away all tears, that if you be innocent you do now shed tears, but if you be guilty that you shall by no means do so.

The tears shed by Christ became an object of devotion and were considered particularly precious. A flask containing one was a recognized and valued relic; the Shroud of Turin was thought to show signs of tears as well as of sweat and blood. Paintings often show the heart of Jesus weeping tears of blood; there is a Mass entitled *De Lacryma Christi* and a famous wine of the same name.

The tears of Mary have been even more honoured. She is often represented as 'Our Lady of Tears' and shown weeping. In this role she is the patroness of Spoleto, a town in Italy. A picture of her painted on a wall was seen to shed tears and a chapel was built on the spot in 1485. There are hundreds of reports of miraculous statues of Mary weeping real tears: some are reported to weep blood. They have been seen in many countries of Europe and in America. In a study of miraculous images of Mary which weep, the author, Father Hebert SM, after saying there is a long history of these writes, 'There has never been such an outpouring of tears as there has been in this century ... more explicitly during the ten years, 1971–1981, particularly so in Italy and in the United States'.

The tears are thought to be caused by her pain as she looks at the sins of the world, and are meant to inspire the watchers to repent and to set an example to others. These entreaties, though modified, come in a direct line from the prophets of the Old Testament. They too drain the vitality out of women's tears and replace them with passivity, penance and guilt. Even the representations of Mary offered by the statues reinforces that image. They uniformly show young, narrow-shouldered, and in so far as one can see through the draperies, narrow-hipped, flat-chested women with long pale hands which have clearly never done a stroke of work. The faces are meek and accepting, the tears trembling gently on the cheeks; one cannot imagine these model women roaring with laughter or howling with rage. In this way the Catholic Church has devitalized and drained of energy the power of those tears and confined women in the church to helplessness.

The joyful energy which women could generate was seen as dangerous, and the Christian church today is often equally suspicious of charismatic services. In the same way it is suspicious of women, and the way in which they can transform tears into a source of erotic and celebratory power that can lead to resurrection. They have been firmly removed from the rituals of power, their role frozen into passive and silent weeping at the foot of the cross where the god has been hung.

But in the Catholic Church, unlike the Protestant churches, they at least have another woman to whom they can pray. In spite of the image of her that is presented, women coming to her know she had a child, and that she suffered. Go into any church in a poor area and you're likely to find candles lit before the statue of Mary and little messages on scraps of paper asking for her help. You may even find a woman in tears.

The churches are ruled by men but kept alive by women. They form the bulk of congregations, raise funds, clean and decorate the churches. It is hard to understand why. One possibility is that, with all its institutional faults, the spiritual church offers some form of communication with that part of women that maintains contact with the power of fertility. They know that even in the often dreary services some attempt, no matter how limited, is being made to make contact with the great mystery.

It is difficult for us today to enter fully into the power that those ancient rituals must have generated, but anyone who has attended a religious revival meeting with its emphasis on repentance, tears and rebirth is in touch with the same forces. These forces cannot be eliminated. Various kinds of religious rituals have carried that creative power through the centuries, but now in the West they are falling into disuse in the orthodox churches. They are being revived in the Third World and in the crusades run by evangelists, which tells us how fundamental these forces are. Religion and tears are inextricably mixed, but often, so is erotic frenzy. In rural areas of America, the young men learned that after a religious revival meeting, the young women attending could be led unprotesting into the fields and bushes behind the evangelical tent. The goddess lives on.

Tears and weeping became a recognized part of spiritual discipline for many mystics. In Catherine of Siena's *Dialogue*, she charts the five stages of weeping the mystic may expect. In the last stage:

> Just as green wood, when it is put into the fire, weeps tears of water in the heat because it is still green (for if it were dry it would not weep), so does the heart weep when it is made green again by the renewal of grace, after the dessicating dryness of selfishness has been drawn out of the soul.

The importance of these spiritual disciplines is also recognized in Islam, where from earliest times there has been a certain class of men known as 'The Weepers', who devote themselves to ascetic practices.

Until the eighteenth century, religion was the only force to speak to the central concerns of human beings, the only explanation for human suffering which was available. From that time on, in the West, increasing human mastery of the world in the form of science offered explanations of disease and of natural catastrophes which weakened the power of the churches and offered alternatives which excited the human imagination. The rise of science coincided with the spread of new values which emphasized independence of individual thought in ways that were essentially a challenge to the power of the churches, their priests and ministers. The scientists could offer better explanations when things went wrong. Germs in the body were easier to accept than God's punishment. More important, you could get medicine guaranteed to cure you, whereas God didn't always answer your prayers. Perhaps most important was the idea that you didn't need to suffer, and much of the importance of religion lay in its claim to make sense of suffering. When science found ways of easing pain, both physical and emotional, most people preferred to abandon rather than understand it. We forget what life must have been like for people without anaesthetics and painkillers.

For more and more people God became an irrelevance except when science didn't yet offer solutions. The great transitions of life – birth, marriage and death – retained their power over the imagination, and the rituals around these are all that have kept many churches functioning. But that functioning is marginal to the lives of most people in affluent societies.

But though the churches are failing, religion is in some ways more powerful than ever, if by 'religion' we mean some way for people to make sense of their lives, and particularly suffering. Not only has science failed to solve all our problems, it is increasingly viewed as a monster which threatens to destroy us and the planet. Even the marvellous triumphs of medicine are losing the preventative health battle to the insidious increase of mysterious allergies, diseases of the environment and psychosomatic illnesses. The political march of reason has halted, and the churches of eastern Europe are packed with worshippers trying to make sense of their lives. Esoteric cults proliferate and many attempts, like astrology, to make links between human lives and the pattern of the universe are attracting new adherents.

Religion is a fundamental source of another quality – compassion. It is not enough to weep for ourselves; we have to be able to weep for others. The Old Testament is one of the great world sources of compassion for the poor and the hurt: the prophets thundered in their defence: 'Oh that my head were waters and mine eyes a fountain of tears, that I might weep day and night for the slain of the daughter of my people' (Jeremiah, 9:1). The New Testament also constantly urges care and compassion not only for the poor, but for all injured people. 'For out of much affliction and anguish of heart I wrote unto you with many tears; not that ye should be grieved, but that ye might know the love which I have more abundantly unto you' (2 Corinthians, 2:4).

Those who believe in the Christian God believe that the cause of suffering lies somewhere in our relationship with that God: part of that relationship lies in our links with other human beings. We cannot live in isolation if we wish to be close to God. We have to see their pain as our pain and their need as our need. The word 'care' comes from the Old English *carian*, to suffer. If we care, we suffer with the other.

It is the churches which have too often failed to live according to the model set for them by Christ. It is true that they set up the great caring institutions for the poor, the handicapped and the sick – forerunners of the welfare state. It is also true that some of these institutions have been run in brutal and insensitive ways, particularly against children given refuge. There is a formidable list of those in religious orphanages and reform schools whose tears were not respected.

To find the benefits of religion, we have to find some way of separating it from the institutions which claim to represent it. The central problem developed when the participatory nature of ritual was destroyed and replaced with a concept of a god who had no need for the feelings of people, who was placed above them in ways that made any behaviour other than worship and penitence irrelevant. This made guilt central to the relationship, built on fear and sterility of feeling. In a state of fear no other feelings can flower.

A new response is growing from women theologians and from radicals seeking liberation for many oppressed people. They reject the role of helplessness and attempt to re-engage and integrate into religious ritual the energy of the feminine psyche. They have a concept of God which embraces the full range of emotional characteristics, a god who is also a goddess. They are creating new rituals of worship which reflect this unity, this wholeness, and in these rituals celebration can be offered of the capacities for weeping, laughter, joy and for creativity. They do not abase themselves in penitence but see themselves in a partnership which accepts responsibility for establishing peace and justice on this planet. They are celebrating the Creation rather than the Fall.

8
Tears and Health

We are tears
Which were never shed.
The cutting ice
Which all hearts dread
We could have melted;
But now its dart
Is frozen into
A stubborn heart.
The wound is closed;
Our power is lost.

Ibsen, *Peer Gynt.*

I wept not, so of stone grew I within.
Dante, *Inferno*, canto XXXIII, 1.49.

The human race has for thousands of years been aware of powerful links between tears and health. Much of the knowledge was and still is intuitive. In myths and dreams tears are seen as magical, turning into flowers, trees and jewels as they fall and bringing heroes back to life. Greek, Roman, Indian, Eskimo, Irish and Scandinavian myths are full of such stories.

Such race memories live on. A Scottish woman whose son was about to have an operation had a dream the night before it was due. She was carrying him as a baby along a valley devoid of vegetation and with high hills on each side. She realized that there were rival armies shooting across the valley from the hill tops. A stray bullet hit and killed the baby. She knelt down and wept and noticed that where the tears fell on the ground, flowers sprang up. She looked at the baby, also drenched in tears, and found he had come back to life.

While we are all born with the capacity to cry, that capacity can be lost. It can be lost for two main reasons. The first is that the environment in which we live is so hostile to our tears that the pain of showing them outweighs the relief we get from letting them flow. The second is that the pain or distress which we could probably relieve by crying, is so powerful, so overwhelming, that it becomes too deep for tears. What happens is that in order to protect ourselves we erect barriers of denial of feeling between us and the pain. We dare not let ourselves make contact with it in case we lose control, and weep and weep without ever stopping.

When we lose the ability to cry, our body is deprived of one of the great protectors against stress. For the major distresses of our lives, grief, fear, anger and embarrassment, the body has a built-in response, both in sounds and activity. Weeping, sobbing, shaking, sweating, even laughing are all able to discharge emotion. If our mind refuses to let our body respond, the feeling stays locked in and can affect all our physical processes. Weeping and sobbing are natural and appropriate responses to grief and our body is designed to provide the capacity and to use it creatively. The blocking of natural functions can damage our health.

There are alternatives which relieve our immediate tension. We can vent anger by shouts and gesticulation. We can get drunk, we can excite ourselves sexually until we achieve an orgasm. But all these alternatives can carry a price more damaging than weeping.

As so often happens, ordinary people and poets recognized this before the scientists. 'Have a good cry', 'I'll feel better once I've had a good cry', 'I'm worried about her, she hasn't shed a tear since she had the news', are all sayings which have a recognized place in our language. Lord Tennyson wrote,

> *Home they brought her warrior dead;*
> *She nor swoon'd nor utter'd cry,*
> *All her maidens, watching, said*
> *'She must weep or she will die'.*

A distinguished psychosomatic physician, Dr A. Cameron Macdonald, documented his own findings on what he describes as the water-retention syndrome. This condition normally gives rise to severe swelling, known as oedema, in various parts of the body. Often this has a clearly organic cause, but there are many cases where no organic explanation can be found and emotional factors have to be considered. Dr Macdonald was consulted on a series of cases which gave him clues to what was to become an accepted theory.

The first was an elderly lady with severe swelling of the eyelids and around the mouth. The story, gently explored, was that this condition began after the death of a sister whom she had failed to visit during her final illness, in spite of having been sent for. Her feelings of grief were complicated by feelings of guilt and she had not wept. She said that in any case, 'she was not given to crying'. Within hours of her sister's death she had developed swelling of the eyelids and face.

The second, whom Dr Macdonald saw the following day, was a young pregnant woman who had developed rapidly increasing oedema, a dangerous symptom in pregnancy. Organic causes were ruled out so, as is his wont, he sat down and talked to her. Her mother had died and her father summoned her to come to him at once. She was caught in a confusion of grief for her mother and guilt about her inability, because of her pregnancy, to make the long journey north which father was demanding. Dr Macdonald cut through the guilt with his paternalistic authority, more power-ful in the hospital than her father's, and insisted that she must stay where she was. This left her free to grieve.

The third patient, encountered the following morning, was a young actor whose face had swollen to the size of a football. Dr Macdonald, alerted by the events of the previous two days, explored the possibility of recent bereavements; all were denied. Then the young man said, 'It depends what you mean by bereave-ments', and went on to describe his conflict about a woman with whom he was in love but not yet ready to marry. She had just told him she was tired of waiting and would find someone else.

Each of these people, when able to confront grief directly, passed great quantities of water through their bladder and the swelling rapidly subsided. A further fifty cases followed up showed a bereavement or separation in forty-six cases and thirty-nine of the forty-six had associated guilt, anger or resentment. The one feature which occurred in almost every case was that patients had been discouraged from showing feeling and especially from weeping in childhood.

In another study of sixty-eight patients suffering from oedema, forty-two patients required only one 'talking' interview for the symptom to subside. The other twenty-six responded to psychotherapy which ranged in length from one month to four years. Of the sixty-eight, only six admitted that they could weep easily and without embarrassment. Dr Macdonald clearly identifies the link between oedema, weeping and the flow of urine from the bladder in which the body frees itself from the water retained in the tissues causing the swelling which brings the patient to the doctor. He demonstrates how when the patient is helped to weep the kidneys can produce sometimes as much as a litre of urine.

Another of Dr Macdonald's encounters was with a woman who suffered, among other things which included slightly swollen ankles, from Sjogren's Syndrome, an extremely uncomfortable state of dry eyes. He wondered if dry eyes might also be a symbolic message about weeping and tears so asked her if she had been allowed to cry as a child. She replied, 'Oh no, I was never allowed to cry and I cannot relieve myself'.

One woman, helped to 'relieve herself', was brought up by a mother who continually told her that, 'Big girls don't cry'. When later attending the funeral of her ten-year-old nephew, she overheard the officiating clergyman say to the child's mother, 'Now you mustn't cry'. She seized the astonished man by the shoulder and said to him, 'Never, ever say that again!'. I would have liked to say that to the normally pleasing Duchess of Kent when shown on television visiting a home for people who are elderly. One old lady, overcome by her situation, burst into tears. The Duchess, obviously finding this very painful, was heard to say, 'Don't cry, please don't cry'. The idea has bitten deeply into our way of life.

The muscles are often the repositories of the tension that tears are not allowed to relieve. The stiff upper lip is a barrier against the trembling which could lead to tears. The stiff neck is a way of controlling feeling as are the rigid shoulders and the pulled-in gut.

Any experienced masseur can tell how often, as they release muscle tension, tears are shed. There are particular muscles which seem to carry most of the burden, and it can take several sessions to help them become relaxed. Crying seems an essential part of the process. Often patients come with considerable back or neck pain, but unless they can use the experience of crying to look at the repression of feeling in their lives, the effects of the massage is short-lived as the tensions quickly build up again.

Teachers of the Alexander technique, concerned about total body posture, become very aware in their own training of the way we hold feelings in our bodies. During their three-year training, which is a combination of theory and practice, it is a normal experience for students, as their bodies recover natural balance, to go through periods of deep and intense weeping after which there is significant improvement in their postural skills. They make no attempt to explore the cause of those tears, concentrating instead on living without muscular tension.

Some forms of psychotherapy are based on the work of Reich, an analyst who gave up 'talking' therapy because he saw the possibility of releasing emotional tension locked into the body, and making faster contact with the sources of conflict that cause pain and distress. He believed that the memory of every experience in our lives is imprinted somewhere in our body tissues, mostly in our muscles, and we can recover those memories by using a series of physical movements, positions and methods of breathing which will restimulate experiences of pain and distress. Dramatic explosions of anger and tears are inevitable consequences of this style of therapy. Anger and tears are opposite faces of the same coin.

Anger which is denied, not allowed into consciousness, or else repressed to just below the level of consciousness, spilling over rarely, is one of the most powerful sources of stress the human body has to cope with. It involves a constant holding-back or a holding-together of the self, and uses enormous energy, as if letting go would be desperately dangerous. This holding-back plays havoc with bodily functions, and research is continually showing us new relationships between stress and our physiology. Connections have been made with, among other illnesses, skin rashes, asthma, heart disease, backache and cancer. More recently we have learnt that the functioning of the immune system, that exquisitely coordinated mechanism protecting us from disease, is intimately tied in to levels of stress.

The ability to cry is one of nature's ways of relieving stress and tension. After a 'good cry', properly in touch with our feelings, there are significant changes in body tone. The body feels and looks 'softer', muscles are more relaxed and skin tone improves. This kind of crying may have to be relearnt by those whose early life experiences have distorted their natural capacity. We are constantly being offered esoteric techniques of relaxation and meditation to counteract stress, yet choose to ignore what is naturally available or are ashamed to use it.

When Professor Cary Cooper, head of Organizational Psychology at the University of Manchester Institute of Science and Technology, published research showing statistical links between breast cancer and stress, he also showed that the women most likely to develop breast cancer were more withdrawn and when they cried tended to cry alone. His advice to stressful women was: 'If you cry, don't cry alone. Do it when other people are around so that someone will see that you are upset and listen to you. If that is too difficult, seek other help – counselling will do you more good than valium'.

After the 1990 Football World Cup offered us images of football heroes bursting into tears as a way of dealing with their despair, Professor Cooper was quoted as saying, 'Crying is a psychological and physical recovery. All the research shows that one of the best coping strategies is to let emotions out, and one of the worst is not to do that. There is growing evidence that bottling up your emotions weakens your immune system'.

In counselling, indeed in any of the 'talking' therapies, tears play an important part, first of all in the release of tension, and later as a way of directing attention to areas which are 'tender' and might repay exploration. They may be the first sign of trust given, an attempt to show an external sign of an internal pain as a way of having it noticed. The counsellor is given an opportunity to treat the pain with respect, and for the person seeking help this can be a supremely important experience. The woman who died of cancer and left the poems expressing her soul's pain written over twenty years of marriage on the kitchen window sill, for her husband to find, was saying that no one in that house had respected her pain sufficiently to share it. In her lifetime she was never known to cry, never known to complain.

Cancer, most feared of illnesses, is now seen to be intimately related to our emotional life. The idea shocked many people who were convinced that the only cause must be genetic, or chemical, or a virus, something they could put under a microscope. These factors may indeed be present but are more likely to act as partners with unresolved emotional issues in people's lives, rather than to initiate the disease. An American study from the University of Oregon showed that housewives had a 54 per cent higher incidence of cancer than the female population as a whole and 157 per cent higher than that portion of the female population who work outside the home. Research workers tried to find carcinogenic materials in kitchens, but further analysis of the data showed that people paid to work in kitchens have less cancer than housewives in spite of spending twice as much time in them. The missing factor was how housewives feel about their lives.

Lack of opportunities to express their feelings is a common factor in the history of cancer patients and the illness may be a response to that. One holistic therapist I know, always asks her patients when taking their history, 'And when did you decide to die?' Frequently they give her the exact day they decided life was not worth living, and sometimes even the time of day the decision was made. Death becomes the way out of deep hurts, the unexpressed griefs and resentments eating away at self over the years.

The most common experiences in the two years before a cancer is diagnosed are a significant loss or a sense of meaninglessness in the whole process of living. This afternoon I am going to a memorial service for a woman who devoted her whole life to caring for others. Nothing was ever too much trouble for her, her job was her life. Two years ago she was forced into early retirement because of cuts in funding to the organization where she worked. A woman who valued herself more could have said, 'Well, now I'll have time to do other things', but for this woman life without the sense of being needed and of other people valuing her had no point. It was her breasts, those symbols of nurturance, that first showed signs of cancer, and from the moment it was diagnosed she resigned herself to her fate. Lovely warm things will be said to-day: she might not be dead if we had said them to her while alive, and let her weep out her hurt and pain at her rejection on our shoulders. But we were all too polite to be honest. Nor did we reflect on the way in which work can be used by some people as a substitute for living an authentic life. They give to others what they want for themselves.

Asthma can be an emotionally-triggered illness closely linked to the inability to cry, and a 'good cry' can frequently avert an attack. Many asthma attacks end when crying begins. In psychotherapy, with patients suffering from asthma, the relief from tension is often associated with dreams of rainfall, most common symbol of tears. The central experience of asthma is the feeling of being stifled and one's breath being trapped. It is as if the person is balanced on a pivot between being angry and bursting into tears, and an honest expression of either feeling relieves the tension. But frequently the asthma sufferer learned to hold back both feelings because neither are acceptable to the family. The drugs prescribed to relieve an attack force the respiratory passages to allow air in and out, but until the conflict about feelings is resolved or another outlet found, attacks will recur.

Tears not shed openly may be shed in other ways. A friend of mine who reached her fortieth birthday without having the child she hoped for, began to bleed severely from her womb. Hormone treatment had no effect. For quite other reasons she joined a women's therapy group, and in the course of the work stumbled into the unrealized intensity of the pain her barrenness was causing. She had protected herself but became aware that her womb was weeping for her. Menstruation has been described as 'the weeping of the disappointed uterus'.

The constantly-dripping nose for which no explanation can be found is another example, the catarrh which never quite clears up, the cold that comes out of the blue when life is difficult for us. If we're able to use it the cold may win us a few days in which to withdraw to bed and grieve gently for ourselves; if not at least we can weep openly at work, blowing our nose and wiping our eyes, and get a little consideration and sympathy from others for our sad lot.

Dr John Harrison, author of *Love Your Disease – it's keeping you Healthy*, claims that sinusitis, particularly in men, often indicates a reluctance to cry. This is a view widely held among alternative and complementary practitioners.

If we cry when we are sad, the physiological response is tears from the eyes and nose. When we've finished being sad, the mucous membranes in the nose and sinuses settle back to the normal uninflamed state. If the sadness is there but not ever directly expressed by crying ... the mucous membranes remain chronically inflamed, never really pouring out mucous and never really resting. Low-grade inflammation results in swollen membranes which eventually block the openings to the sinuses, causing pain and further discharge. This is chronic sinusitis.

Dr Harrison, who places stress on the importance of looking closely at his patients, watches eyes and eyelid margins to see if they are red or swollen. If so he wonders if the patient needs to cry and has for some reason stopped himself.

There are reports of links between crying and urticaria, a rash resembling nettle rash. Several researchers in psychosomatic medicine have reported cases where attacks of urticaria ended when the patient wept and returned when weeping was repressed. It has been accepted that suppressed anger is a powerful force in skin rashes, and again the link between expressing anger and expressing grief comes into play. The symbolism of weeping eczema seems obvious.

All illnesses carry symbolic meanings as well as the purely physiological. We may have a genetic pre-disposition to cancer, but where or when it appears in our body is determined by a combination of factors. There is an increasing sense that each person's life-history plays a part in the illness 'chosen' by the body. We speak of someone who is stiff-necked long before they may become crippled with arthritis. The patient with back pain will say, 'I'm scared stiff'. The illness and the personality are linked. Some people's rashes are entirely hidden by their clothes: they put 'a good face' on it. Other people who get psoriasis only on knees and elbows may need to fend people off. We talk casually of someone drowning in work or drinking themselves to death long before a terminal illness shows itself or their suicidal drive is detected. We may not ask for help by weeping, but our bodies may become helpless so that we have to be helped. We may not have the courage to scream for attention but we can ensure, by being ill, that we get it.

The awful triumvirate of fear, guilt and anger has to be faced and the tension built up in the body dealt with. The gut, the liver, the bowel, the circulatory and nervous systems are all intimately responsive to these emotions. None of these emotions can be separated from the other; they are linked in ways not clearly understood. It helps to bring them into consciousness and accept them. The way we handle feelings about illnesses, we now know, will have a considerable effect on the capacity to recover from them. Some people succumb without a struggle. Increasingly, others are looking to understand the message their body is giving them and learn from it. Fear may be equally distributed between both sexes, but guilt is usually nearer the surface in women, while anger is more likely to be nearer the surface in men.

These are socially conditioned responses. Some people can struggle by themselves to understand and learn new and more creative ways of living. Others may want someone to work with them and there is a wide range of therapies available. Not all therapies are suited for all people. Some can be damaging. If, for many years, tears have been frozen in order to protect us from intense pain, the process of thawing out may require great delicacy and sensitivity. If unleashed too suddenly, the pain can overwhelm us and we may feel it too much to endure. So the choice of the person with whom we share this personal journey has to be made with great care. Profound feelings need to be experienced in an atmosphere of safety, respect and integrity.

Academic qualifications, while they can be an important guide, cannot be the only criteria. Therapists should be interviewed and their views on issues important to you in other areas of your life examined. Do they have sexist, ageist or racist attitudes that might emerge at a critical point in your work together? How democratic is their style and is that important to you? Could you work more effectively with a male or female therapist? What happens if, in the middle of therapy, you lose your job and can't keep up the fees? Too many people entrust their psyche to a therapist with less thought than they take when finding a garage to service their car.

Acute emotional pain is a powerful threat. Fear is our most primitive and important response. Tears and anger flow back and forward and round fear, fear for our survival, fear of rejection, fear of loss of dignity and of life. Tears may start with howls of anger, then subside to sobs which seek attention for distress, and finally dry up in fear as we face our helplessness. Now we are overtaken by guilt, and the pain of fear and helplessness is interpreted as punishment for nameless sins. We don't know what we have done to deserve our fate, but we must have done something. The adult response of reason is swept away to reveal the small child cowering under parental wrath. These are some of the feelings we may have to explore if we seek not to be victims of our emotional life.

CHOICES

Some therapies replay these early experiences by using drama, art and music to make contact with deeper layers of awareness than are normally available. Working with a dramatherapist, we can become an outraged, authoritarian father or a rebellious daughter using words written by Shakespeare 400 years ago about situations which have as much meaning to-day as they did then. In *A Midsummer Night's Dream*, Hermia's father Egeus complains to the king, saying,

> *Full of vexation come I, with complaint*
> *Against my child, my daughter Hermia . . .*
> *As she is mine, I may dispose of her . . .*

To which Hermia later replies with the well-known plea of the young for understanding, 'I would my father looked but with my eyes'.

Having been drawn into the awareness, having re-experienced it in our bodies, we can then stand outside it and see what its meaning is for us. Dr Sue Jennings, a pioneer in dramatherapy, described how an infertile woman may learn to identify sorrow and rage against the sterile womb which, every month, rejects the fertilized egg: how she can move from passive grief to weeping rage in which she pounds her belly with her hands, railing against its refusal to give a home to the child she desperately wants. And somehow, having made contact with the deepest part of herself, the woman often gives permission to that womb to flower.

In this way, protected by a structure created by a skilled therapist, we can cower in fear, howl with anger, weep with panic, rend our clothes in guilt and let go any need to hold on to feelings which belong to our past rather than our present lives. We may not have known that they lay beneath the surface of our lives. Until we do know, we cannot give them expression in tears or anger. This process of catharsis can bring improvements in both physical and mental health. In a variety of forms it was known in ancient times. Aristotle wrote about it in relation to drama and what we can gain by going to the theatre. It is a recognized component of rituals of healing we can still see being practiced by the wise men, witch doctors and shamans in 'primitive' societies and sometimes in the spiritual healing work of evangelical preachers.

Another well-known form of therapy, co-counselling, relies heavily on catharsis. Using a democratic structure of rotating the roles of therapist and patient, it encourages people to express previous hurts in ways they might have done as children if that had been allowed. Tears, weeping, sobbing, shaking and reliving the experiences which triggered off these powerful feelings, leave the person being counselled exhausted after a session but peaceful, and often with a new perception of the world. The founder of co-counselling, Harvey Jackin, along with other therapists like Dr Janov, best known for his work on the Primal Scream, believes that only by re-experiencing the pain locked away in the psyche, repressed by not being allowed the simple physiological responses of weeping and crying, can that pain be eliminated from the system. When the capacity to express powerful feeling is restored, changes occur not only in the person's perception of the world but also in their physiology. Janov details changes in tension headaches, heart rates, blood pressure, skin disorders, stomach disorders and much else. He argues that all other forms of therapy are simply tranquillizers, helping people to adapt rather than change, or else to find an addiction like meditation or relaxation that offers temporary relief to which we will always need to return.

Other people may find more low-key but equally powerful ways of working with their thoughts and feelings, gaining insight into the causes of their distress. At different stages of life, different forms of therapy may be helpful. When we have left behind the turbulence of adolescence and shed some of the more harrowing demands of responsibility for making careers and caring for the next generation, we may seek opportunities to assess our lives and face its later stages with some serenity. For this, the work of Carl Jung has offered some of the most creative wisdom.

Health, emotional and physical, and ways of achieving it, have replaced arguments about religion and spiritual salvation. In a secular society, where death no longer holds out hope of an after-life and heaven, the quality of the life we know we have has assumed an importance previously given to the life of the soul. Argument about rival therapies has taken on the passion previously given to theological debate. Health has integrated the concepts of sin and guilt. If all these books written about our power to influence our health by right action and right thinking are true, then to be sick is our own fault and we should feel guilty. The appeal to doctrines of reincarnation is an almost essential fall-back as it shifts the burden of full responsibility from our shoulders.

It seems essential that such a burden should be shared. Few people are capable of bearing the full and stark responsibility for their fate. In recent years we have seen the most thorough pursuit ever carried out to find partners in responsibility for the ailments to which we are subject. Food plays a particularly important part. Fantasies of being poisoned, so often a feature we carry into adult life from the inevitable conflicts of infancy, are the most common, although pollution offers a reality base for our fears. Our lethargy, our depression, our eczema, our lumps, our arthritis, our coronaries, our aches and pains, our allergies, are entirely due to polluted food . . . say some. Others with equal cogency argue that damage to our health lies in our failure to take exercise, or in some form of faulty body co-ordination that constricts important pathways for our nerves, veins and arteries.

Much of this is undoubtedly true but perhaps not true enough to justify the industries springing up all over the country offering simplistic solutions like food supplements and gymnasia. The more responsible therapists, like acupuncturists, reflexologists, yoga teachers and herbalists, offer interesting and usually sensible explanations for symptoms. The backaches, the headaches, the abdominal pressure, the fatigue and skin troubles as well as the life threatening illnesses for which no cure is on tap from conventional medicine often respond to these alternative or complementary therapies ... for a time. Then, to the disappointment of both therapist and patient, the improvement halts and fades away and the patient moves on to try something else, blaming either themselves or the therapist.

There are some remarkable examples of genuine healing, but increasingly these are seen to be linked with some inner process involving a drive to self-healing. It is this new emphasis that causes such anxiety and guilt to those for whom self-healing does not work. Do I really not want to be well? the cancer sufferer asks herself. Do I really hate my life or myself so much that I want to die?

The answers involve asking ourselves every time we are ill, what benefits that illness brings us. It is not an easy question and sometimes there is more than one answer. One is, however, fairly constant: the pain and discomfort of illness is frequently easier than the other kind of pain and hurt in our unconscious memories. The demons of early agony of being abandoned when left alone for longer than we could bear it, the terror of being annihilated by a raging adult, the suffocating experience of being trapped in the tunnel of our mother's body with a cord tightening round our neck ... it is hard to face those feelings again. It is easier to keep them buried, push the feelings back down with stiffened muscles, joints and tension headaches.

We can withdraw into fatigue. One fascinating interaction between mind and body is seen in an illness known as psycho-somatic glycaemia fatigue. The symptoms are excessive fatigue, either in the form of chronic or acute attacks. What identified sufferers was a collapse of motivation. They forced themselves to keep going but they had no enthusiasm. Some had lost faith in their marriage, some in hope for promotion, some on discovering that they would never have a child. The physical result of this apathy and lack of zest was an inability to raise the sugar concentration in the blood. The conclusion is that we need enthusiasm for living to be healthy and energetic. To retain enthusiasm in the face of difficulties, we must receive respect for our tears and complaints in childhood and be helped to renew hope when facing difficulties.

We are swamped to-day with books and articles about the power of positive thought to heal our physical or our emotional ills. Dr Coué, who, in the nineteenth century proclaimed the virtue of saying first thing every morning and regularly thereafter that, 'Every day, in every way I'm getting better and better', is enjoying a great revival. The phrases used are different but the message is the same, 'I approve of myself', 'I am a child of the Universe', 'I relax and trust in life'. It's quite hard work for some of us to take this seriously, but that may be because we are not very good at loving ourselves or trusting life. What is important is the discovery that saying these things can actually make us feel better, but only if we say them with sincerity. Saying positive things about ourselves or having positive things said to us actually produces a chemical response in our brains. Holding the idea that we are good, that we are lovable, that we are cared for, seems to act in much the same way as a tranquillizer. The idea enters the brain and by being given meaning triggers off a biochemical process which soothes and makes us feel happy. Being stroked physically has the same soothing effect and the phrase, 'being stroked' when we are complimented grows from the similarity of these experiences.

By having someone in our adult lives who constantly feeds us verbal tranquillizers, or by feeding them to ourselves we can ease emotional pains and keep them at bay for a while. But if the pain is rooted in our past and is never brought into consciousness, we will need stronger and stronger doses of the tranquillizer. It is when these fail that sex, drugs or alcohol are invoked to more effectively push down the pain. Actors and politicians use applause, fanatical followers of cults, religions or political parties use a different set of ideas, which can range from love for one's fellow human beings to projections of bitter hate upon one's enemies. The leaders become very skilled at giving their followers a range of 'fixes' to meet their need to be valued, but also their need to have someone to hate.

Most of us will try anything to ease ourselves of the pain of having been unsatisfactory children. We will seek reassurance that we are loved in all kinds of bizarre ways rather than acknowledge there were times when we were not loved, or we may never have been loved, or even that we may have been hated. We may seek out partners incapable of loving us in the way we need so as to experience again the brief hope that this time it will be all right or as Lisa Minelli sang in the film *Cabaret*, 'This time I'll be lucky', before the pain sweeps in again to overwhelm us.

Most of us will try anything rather than face the pain, yet that is the only way out of it, and tears and weeping are an essential factor in the cure. Every therapist of emotional pain, no matter their particular style, sees the discharge of feeling through tears as a positive and healing experience. Most see it as essential, preferably happening in the company of the therapist but sometimes taking place in between therapeutic sessions. Weeping in therapy sessions, say some, can be used as a defence against having to talk about the pain. It can go on and on, soaking through boxes of tissues, seemingly having no end and making it quite impossible for the patient to speak or to say why he is crying. This can last for some weeks. Other therapists would say that this weeping is an expression of pain experienced in the life of the person before words were available.

Weeping serves two purposes. One cleanses the brain of the chemicals associated with depression which in turn gives rise to feelings of sorrow. The second is to release emotional tension. This effect is temporary unless the feeling which is linked with the tears can be experienced: therapists would say re-experienced, since the deep pain triggering the tears is seldom about experiences happening in our day-to-day lives. It is more likely to be about sore things from childhood, which we were not allowed properly to experience or mourn: or we may have been too young in emotional or physical development to cope.

Children who have had happy, loving and stable early experiences will when hurt simply weep for a while to relieve the hurt, then get on with life. They will not need to overreact with despair or anger. For some it may be that the act of crying was left free for them to use in a healthy way. Freud and Breur described one case which illustrates this capacity for self-healing. The woman they described had nursed three or four people whom she loved, through a final illness. Each time she exhausted herself but managed never to become ill. What happened was that after each death she would go through a process of remembering the scenes of illness and death.

Every day she would go through each impression once more, would weep over it and console herself – at her leisure one might say. This process of dealing with her impressions was dovetailed into her everyday tasks without the two activities interfering with each other. In addition to these outbursts of weeping with which she made up arrears and which followed close upon the fatal termination of the illness, the lady celebrated annual festivals of remembrance at the period of the various catastrophes.

This contrasts sadly with the experience of an elderly woman I met who suffered three bereavements in quick succession. All were people whom she loved deeply, one was her husband, the other her son, the third her sister. She told me that after the second, her son's death, she was so angry with God that she refused to cry and found after her sister's death, she was unable to. She now had a permanent pain in her chest which she knew quite clearly was related to her inability to cry. She knew also that it would not clear until she could recover her tears.

For most people their tears are distorted in some way or another, often confused and strangled, not flowing freely. It is very unusual in 'advanced' societies for us to cry without at the same time apologizing. An important aspect of these therapies is that people are given permission to cry and are guided through the experience. For the rest of us crying is a hit or miss experience, sometimes satisfying but sometimes leaving us drained, exhausted or more hopeless than when we started.

This probably relates to our reason for crying and the early history of how our tears were responded to. One man, told by his doctor that he had cancer, retreated to his bedroom and wept for a week, refusing to eat and waiting to die. He fell back into the pattern of helplessness in the face of distress that he had been taught in the cradle. There was no fairy godmother to rescue him. Another person could weep and out of the weeping find memories of strengths which could lead to formulating a treatment plan and a cure.

The most healing tears are those which neither overwhelm us with pain, nor are so detached from our feelings that we do not really own them. Ideally we should both feel the pain and also retain awareness of what is happening. The most successful weepers are those who have integrated a loving carer into their experience, so that even when they are weeping alone they do not feel abandoned or frightened. Not all of us have had those good experiences, but we can recapture in later life what we did not find in childhood. We need not be ashamed of borrowing such a carer, either in formal therapy or informal friendship. In experiences of communal disaster or of shared pain we can gain support from those who suffer with us. Tears are magical bcause they can transform us. They can calm, restore, comfort and relieve us. The lesson is to value our own and other people's tears as a source of health, strength and courage.

9

The Tears of Existence

If the Earth were only a few feet in diameter, floating a few feet above a field somewhere, people would come from everywhere to marvel at it. People would walk around it, marvelling at its big pools of water, its little pools and the water flowing between the pools. People would marvel at the bumps on it, and the holes in it, and they would marvel at the very thin layer of gas surrounding it and the water suspended in the gas. The people would marvel at all the creatures walking around the surface of the ball, and at the creatures in the water. People would declare it precious because it was the only one, and they would protect it so that it would not be hurt. The ball would be the greatest wonder known, and the people would come to behold it and be healed, to gain knowledge, to know beauty and to wonder how it could be. People would love it and defend it with their lives, their own roundness could be nothing without it. If the Earth were only a few feet in diameter.

Anon

WEEPING FOR THE WORLD

A new form of suffering was born in this century. It is pain for the world, pain for our planet and for the future of all forms of life. We are the first members of our race who are consciously destroying our own life-support system. And we are the first generation which cannot take it for granted that other generations will follow.

There are some people who openly weep for the threat our world faces, but are thought eccentrics rather than prophets. This is a pain not talked about. It is expressed in privacy, sometimes following a particular experience of mystery and beauty that triggers our sense of vulnerability, the birth of a baby or the sense of awe when viewing the world from the top of a mountain. These are a source of joy but that we might destroy the source of that joy is good cause for tears.

There are parents who wake weeping with nightmares of seeing their children incinerated in a nuclear war but will rarely put their most private fears into public words. They write poems to ease themselves but do not share them. Peace activists learn by rote the facts of the number of nuclear weapons required to destroy the world, they show that already we have 200 times more than is necessary. They can detail the number of computer errors a year which could have triggered a disaster (100 at the last count), but seldom speak of personal rage, terror and sorrow. It is sometimes too much to bear or to share.

Members of Greenpeace and other ecological groups almost bully us with detailed information about the destruction of the rain forests, about acid rain, nuclear waste, the hole made in the Earth's protective layer by our use of aerosols and fossil fuels, the deserts ordinary farmers are making as they crop and burn land. They make us know facts as if somehow knowing facts forces us to do something about it. We distance ourselves from these terrible facts. Some people get out their cheque books, others stuff a pound note or a fiver into an envelope and send a donation but most of us say, 'Isn't that terrible', and feel helpless.

Many are blocked by a confusing mixture of fear, rage and guilt. Some fear about nuclear war comes from knowing we will have to watch helplessly what happens to those we love. Adult love is mixed with a protective tenderness which demands the right to help when we are needed. To be denied that possibility, particularly with one's children, is terrifying. The rage comes from helplessness allied to a sense of the stupidity and pointlessness of the threatened disasters and the messiness and meanness of the world in which we live. We are not victims of invaders from an alien planet. There are no external enemies in whose interest it is to destroy us. We are our own executioners, we are the mindless vandals.

There lies the guilt. We have allowed this to happen and can't understand how we drifted into this crisis. We don't even know how we could have stopped it. Hiroshima, at the time, was just another bomb, a bit bigger certainly. Aerosol cans were a marvellous discovery; nuclear energy was going to give us cheap electricity. How were we to know how bad it was?

It is all too much to believe – particularly that the planet could be destroyed. Our psyche, that part of us which provides the motive force to keep alive, simply refuses to believe we are going to die. It daren't, because if it did, we would simply lie down and never do anything again. It is essential, in order to function at all, that we believe ourselves to be immortal. Even those who say they believe that they will die in a nuclear blast, don't really. We secretly think we will survive even if our children, family and friends are destroyed.

We must find ways of functioning in the world, of behaving as if we could rely on the continuity of the planet, as if our children and grandchildren are going to grow up and have children. We have to plan for the future, for our holidays next year and for retirement in ten years and we have to help our children do the same. They have to think it worth while to learn their tables and do homework. Over millions of years most human beings have acquired the skill not to think of unpleasant things unless they are actually happening. This means tucking unacceptable knowledge into a back pocket of our minds, keeping it in a separate compartment and trying to ignore it. Personal suffering is hard enough to face: a true perception of cosmic suffering is intolerable. Those people who work with weapons of destruction or who have some responsibility for their use would go mad if they allowed themselves to feel the horror that would be unleashed on the world. Their sanity depends on the capacity to deny the truth.

As the years pass and the horrors grow, an increasing number of people suffer from what Robert Lifton, who studied Hiroshima survivors, called 'psychic numbing'. We simply shut down awareness so we can continue to watch television, we can continue to read newspapers but no longer respond with real feeling. We say the words, 'Isn't that terrible', but we cut ourself off from the feeling. We are no longer weeping even at secondhand. But feelings don't disappear if the causal factors don't disappear; they hold on to energy. They linger in the basement of our lives, seeking forms of expression, a pool of anxiety emerging in dreams or odd forms of behaviour. We can have dreams of violence and death, we can engage in pointless attempts to give meaning to our lives by extravagant spending, athletic sexuality or an obsession with appearance or status.

There are among us a few who react differently and more creatively. They seek ways to stop the madness of global destruction. For every one person who reacts so directly, there are many thousands who less dramatically support them and are grateful for their single-mindedness. The few are living out the sorrow, the hopes and aspirations of the many. This is seen in Peace Camps where people live outside weapon bases. Greenham, maintained only by women, has had most publicity and been a great source of learning. But the other Peace Camps in places like Faslane, and a number of communities of like-minded people scattered around the country are making an equally important contribution. Trying to find new and more creative ways for humans to live together, they handle feelings by confronting rather than denying them. Tears, fear, anger, love, anything except violence is accepted. Feelings which in the wider society would be shameful and not shared are acknowledged and respected. Their lives bear witness to their beliefs, and pain is transformed through being expressed in the world and acted on creatively. Their resultant capacity to laugh and celebrate is a great strength. They have much to teach us.

New ways are emerging to help people cope creatively with their pain for the world. The best known are the despair workshops. Begun in America but now found in many countries, they attempt to work with the despair that participants bring to the workshop. Their intention is to convert the energy locked in despair to a sense of power used in social action. This is done by sharing feelings. Each person involved allows themselves to enter fully into the pain from which previously they protected themselves. Despair can be a form of defence. The pain and later the power are evoked by using a number of techniques drawn from religious and psychological sources ... drawing, dancing, chanting, guided daydreams, meditation. In the evocation of the pain, the full range of fear, grief, rage and guilt is experienced through tears, weeping and distress. The empowerment grows from this catharsis.

The women's peace movement experiments with similar ideas at protest meetings. By singing, dancing and using symbolism they evoke feeling and power. The fences of the bases are transformed with flowers and photographs and clothing of small children as a way of making contact with tenderness and vulnerability. At one Scottish demonstration by grandmothers, a cardboard cutout of a child was covered with the names of their grandchildren and laid on the ground. Forming a circle round it, the women read a litany linking themselves to their femininity and to grandmothers in other countries. Even the women police guarding their activity were moved to tears. The action ended by handing the cutout into the Ministry of Defence police guarding the base.

What is important is that these ideas should not lead to self-indulgent exercises of group fervour, either of despair or of ecstacy. Power cannot be experienced in a vacuum, it requires an arena and action, and a goal. If personal power is experienced fully, something has to change and be seen to change. Ceremonies have to take place in public. Carmen Rojas, who runs a women's centre in Chile, a country that has seen great suffering, always says that pain has to be taken out into the world, not held secretly in the heart. Only then can it be transformed. This is the basic premise of the non-violent direct action groups who work in the peace movement.

The group processes described are not very different from processes of individual therapy, nor are they significantly different from religious revival meetings. What does distinguish them is whether or not the participants can move from the private to the public arena. There is a key point where such a shift can take place, where it is not enough to feel better in oneself or to solve one's own problems, but it is essential to take the new power out to change the world. To make change happen we have to protest about the way things are now and show our feelings.

What politicians in power fear most is the expression of strong feelings by members of the public except for those feelings they themselves inspire and feel able to control, like patriotism or party loyalty. For the state, the ideal citizen is modest, sober, hardworking, thrifty and moderate in all his views: a follower of Apollo rather than Dionysius. Public passion is unacceptable and suspect, just as it was to our parents when we yelled with distress.

> I have set before you life and death, blessing and cursing; therefore
> choose life, that both thou and thy seed may live.
>
> Deuteronomy, 30:19.

WEEPING IN POVERTY

'I'm frightened if I let out the pain it will destroy me', she said and burst into tears.

Woman living in a poverty-stricken housing estate.

People living in deprived communities have much in common with those suffering fear and despair about the future of the world. Every country has a significant group of people who live their suffering daily. They are not all peasants in economically-underdeveloped countries. Many are urban poor living in poverty in the midst of an affluent society, a group known as the Fourth World. In London, where shops sell children's party dresses costing more than the average weekly wage, many children are undernourished and living desperate lives in bed-and-breakfast hostels because their parents can find no decent housing.

In Glasgow, the Cultural City of Europe in 1990, poverty caused by lack of jobs rots human lives. Desolate housing estates drag down the human spirit so that energy that could go into work and positive living experiences deteriorates into vandalism, querulousness, jealousy, loss of dignity and self respect. Family life is permeated with anxiety about every aspect of daily routines, the buying of food, the heating of the home, the care of the children, the risk of young people getting into trouble with the police. Attempts to work together to improve the conditions of their lives can be destroyed by the weight of tension and stress people carry daily. One community worker said, 'People bring the stress in which they're living into a committee. So they "fuck" and "blind" and go back home to stress as well. They go back to fighting with their husbands or with their children. The middle class have a support network, the poor have only a sense of helplessness'.

It is not surprising that in these areas little attention is paid to the wider suffering that goes on in the world. Individuals and families have less feeling to spare for what they see as second-order problems. For some of them, the thought that we might be incinerated by nuclear weapons could be a relief or a justified punishment to the affluent for their uncaring. If your heart is full of bitter injustice, if the area where you live is polluted by neglected housing, public squalor, vandalism and drug-peddling, it is hard to focus on what goes on in far-flung places. If the only world you know is physically ugly, how can you weep for the loss of beauty? If you have never had the opportunity to travel beyond the borders of your own city, how can you comprehend the planet? If every time you watch television you are reminded by advertisements, documentaries and soap operas of your isolation and exclusion from the wider society, how can you have a sense of the wholeness and interconnectedness of the planet?

Poverty is a great enemy to human happiness; it certainly destroys liberty, and it makes some virtues impracticable and others extremely difficult.

Samuel Johnson

In a society which glorifies achievement and competition, people often blame themselves if they fail. No one wants to display their poverty so social contacts shrink between unemployed families and those still in jobs. Both groups are embarrassed. How can you enjoy showing holiday snaps from Ibiza to a friend who hasn't been able to do more than take the children to the local park for a picnic? The affluent therefore avoid the poor. They don't want to feel guilty – a very uncomfortable feeling – and conclude in self-defence that it is their fault that they are unemployed. 'Surely', they will say, 'they could do something to help themselves'. The unemployed will also avoid the affluent as their lives become increasingly shameful in their own eyes, unable to keep up patterns of buying clothes, going out for an occasional meal or standing someone a drink in the pub. They do not like their own feelings of resentment, no matter how understandable. Such feelings reinforce a sense of failure and increase feelings of helplessness and powerlessness. Television becomes the main source of stimulation or 'passing the time', now available day and night. At any time, in street after street of dreary housing estates one can see through windows the flickering light and a hunched figure in the chair watching. People isolate themselves, only venturing out when absolutely necessary. They are taking flight from the pain of their lives.

For animals, the response to stress is either flight or fight, but for human beings, neither is particularly helpful. We are not animals. We have the capacity to understand feelings, but we do not use that sufficiently nor teach our children. If anything, we teach them to ignore those feelings. So we should not be surprised if some people under the stress of poverty, particularly the young, will fight: but they cannot fight the true causes of their stress – the unemployment, the lack of stimulation, the frustration. They are more likely to turn to vandalism, gang fighting or petty crime.

If fight seems impossible or unacceptable, as it is to most women, the old, and the more cautious members of the community, they take flight. The only place for most to flee to is inside their heads – in wishful thinking, day dreaming – or into a bottle or a jar of pills. For some who try to avoid such solutions illness may be a respectable alternative. Feelings of fear, anger, despair are denied and because the capacity to feel is indivisible, positive, cooperative and loving feelings are also lost to them.

Stein Ringen in his book *The Possibility of Politics* describes research showing that the more prosperous a community, the more likely people are to participate in social and political life. Other research shows that such confident groups are also more likely to have the capacity to draw on a range of emotions none of which totally overwhelms them. They can be angry while holding on to reason. They can be unhappy and weep without feeling suicidal, they can fail and pick themselves up again. For anyone living under constant stress, as are people in poverty, the moderate response is harder to achieve. If results are not immediate, there is no hope; good and bad are more sharply defined, experience makes trust risky.

Groups of people who live in even a modest degree of affluence, are able to buy themselves out of a range of anxieties. Travelling with small children, for example, is a much simpler exercise if one can bundle them into the back of a car, throwing mackintoshes into the boot in case it rains. The alternative of getting coats on to sometimes rebellious small bodies, walking to the bus stop carrying bags, waiting, getting children and possibly a pushchair on to the bus, keeping them happy on a crowded bus and after reaching one's destination knowing you have to do the whole thing in reverse is exhausting for anyone. If you're also short of money, you're driven to the edge of toleration. Then tearful children, responding to the parent's stress, are more likely to be slapped than comforted. This is only one of a range of situations where money makes life simpler, like paying for help to clean the house and do the ironing, both physically demanding jobs especially when combined with child care; being able to afford the good-quality prepared foods or well-designed clothes in Marks and Spencers; employing baby sitters who make relaxation and adult contacts possible.

These examples relate to parents of young children, one of the most highly-stressed groups in any community, but the theory is equally relevant to people who are elderly and disabled and those caring for them . . . in fact to any human being. The financial ability to use taxis, telephones, restaurants, dry cleaners, offers a way of buying out of stress. They are particularly important for women who have placed on them the responsibility and the anxiety for so much of the detail of living.

In communities where distress and suffering is the norm rather than the exception, weeping is not readily available as a release. Among the unskilled and semi-skilled, the roles of men and women are more sharply defined. For the public face men are tough and macho in style, women submissive. In the private face, women are strong, men an extra child in the family but with special privileges. It is impossible for the women to truly weep for their existential distress. They say they would never stop, so better not start. Where weeping is seen it betokens a classic depression rather than spontaneous and helpful shows of feeling. But since sorrow and pain constantly lie beneath the surface of their lives, they surface through the classical route of sentimentality and tears about matters unconnected with the real pain. Alcohol is a common trigger. Under its influence strong men weep on each other's shoulders for the sorrows of the world, their country, city, or football team. The women weep for their innocence. They thought life was going to be different. But as the pointlessness and ineffectiveness of sentimental tears to relieve the true source of pain becomes evident, the feeling shifts quickly to anger – not used in ways that can change lives, but turned against husbands, children or neighbours.

The social service departments find it very difficult to work in these communities. The 'client' is almost invariably a woman, since it is women who are expected by their husbands to negotiate with the official world. This is another example of the shifting of anxiety on to the least powerful. Social workers are also mostly women so in a majority of cases we have professional women managing poor women. If the status between the women was equal, 'management' might be abandoned for sisterhood.

Conventional ways of working ignore the fact that most poor women are brilliant managers of small amounts of money. They use skills of juggling, sharing, borrowing, postponing payment, then in the nick of time finding an extra bit of money that would make them fortunes if their arena was the Stock Exchange rather than the local shops. And unlike the social worker who is advising them, they manage without credit cards or knowing they can have an overdraft if it is needed. In addition they negotiate and keep the peace in families with a grievous lack of space and comforts. Quarrelling with their husbands may be routinely necessary to get some kind of fairer distribution of resources between the family, the pub or the bookie.

In encounters with social workers very little real weeping takes place. If it starts, the box of Kleenex is whipped out by the worker and a silent, urgent message passed: 'Please don't cry, I really can't cope with that'. This is probably true. If we let ourselves be moved by the sorrows endured by the families of the poor we would have to weep with them. And what would happen to the other seven families waiting to see the social worker that day? But who is to say that it might not be the most loving and helpful thing to do? The worker's need to hold back tears simply confirms expectations of what to expect from authority. For the worker who holds out the Kleenex and says kindly but firmly, 'Here, dry your eyes', it is another stone in the wall of defence against pain she is building round her heart.

Community workers don't expect people to weep. They understand very well the nature and intensity of the pain that exists in communities but have no way of dealing with it on an individual basis. They believe that group action is important, not an individual's responses. What they hope for is that individual pain, when shared, will generate anger and energy necessary to bring about change at a local and national level. What, too often, they fail to see is that creative rather than destructive responses to pain can only come when contact is consciously made with the sadness which underlies anger. It is awareness of the underlying sadness of the human condition that links us to each other. It is the failure to realize this that has converted so much revolutionary success into a renewed oppression and caused the destruction of the high ideals of revolutionary intention.

The effects of constant stress reduce the capacity to cope with the minutiae of daily life. Depression and anxiety are the most common responses for women, particularly those with small children. Depression comes where there is a sense that nothing you can do, no amount of protest can bring about change. Anxiety comes when you never know where the next blow of fate is coming from and are always trying to dodge it. The only source of help is often the local doctor who tends, since he knows the stress in the face of which he feels helpless, to give traditional mood-altering drugs. Many women need ever increasing doses of tranquillizers and anti-depressants. One effect of these is to dry up their tears. Groups to help them overcome dependency on these drugs find that rediscovering the ability to cry is one of the signs that they are recovering. Men who take refuge from their depression or anxiety in a bottle are ignored until their liver collapses or they have delirium tremens. Psychological help is something for the middle classes who have problems that are 'really' emotional rather than worries about how to pay an electricity bill.

There have been some attempts to confront and transform the pain of the community. Some of the most imaginative emerged in Scotland. The Craigmillar Festival Society began in a desperately deprived Edinburgh housing estate of that name. It was described as 'Festival' in defiant and gentle guying of the international high-class festival of music, drama and the arts which attracts massive finance and wealthy middle-class patrons to Edinburgh every year. It was started by a local woman, Helen Crummy, who stays deeply in touch with the power of personal and community pain and suffering. In this kind of area it is easier initially to put people in touch with community suffering than to confront the personal. For Mrs Crummy, the arts, music, painting, poetry and drama were the focus for expressing that suffering. Through that exploration, bringing into consciousness the history of their own community, the local people recognized their own strengths, capacity to survive and the way in which they had retained the ability to weep, laugh and to create life and joy out of the most unlikely situations. In celebrating these capacities through the arts they learnt how to transmute pain into creativity. In time the Festival Society widened its scope to provide counselling and supportive services which examined the individual suffering of members of the community: but the central idea that through artistic experience people's lives can be transformed, was never abandoned. Every attempt has been made to break down isolation, to substitute cooperation for competition and to temper endurance with the capacity for joy.

Other organizations have drawn inspiration from Craigmillar but few have been so successful in gaining support from the local authority, as was the case in Edinburgh. Their flexible, intuitive, spontaneous, 'feminine' style is very different from that of the average local authority. Emphasis is placed on the importance of human feelings. The pain of the lives of people forced to live in areas of deprivation is dramatized, photographed, and written and sung about. But so is their joy, their capacity to work in cooperation with others, their creativity. The first is recognized and respected and that makes possible the celebration of the second. To celebrate one's strengths is a liberating experience. For many it is the first step to self-respect, which has to depend on feeling you have something to give.

Human beings have learned, falteringly, to work together in

families, groups and communities, but as the number of people we interact or negotiate with grows, cooperation becomes more difficult and paranoia grows. We are most effective when we see the face and look into the eyes of the person with whom we work. It helps if the other person speaks the same language, looks reasonably like ourselves, has the same colour of skin and hair and uses the same styles of body language, so that we don't have to cope with the confusion of meanings of messages. It is an advantage if we share common symbols and common gods or other interpretations of the history and meaning of the world and the universe.

We have a global problem, not only of nuclear weapons, not only of pollution, but also of the gross inequality of wealth throughout the world, both within and between nations. There are also differences in attitudes to women, in child rearing practices, sexual behaviour, in attitudes to war, to power, to religion, to racism – even over the use of alcohol. There are differences in language, in styles of dress, in colour of skin. It is surprising that we are not all at each others' throats all the time. But we do have something in common, namely the human capacity to feel sorrow and anger, to own our pain. There is no society in which these feelings are not central. What separates us is the range of defences we use to protect ourselves from sorrow and pain.

These defences cannot be breached by force. The more strongly we attack, the more they resist. Only by opening ourselves to pain and being undefended can we discover that far from being our enemy, it can be our most powerful ally. Through tears we can find the route to our full humanity. An awareness of our need to weep together could offer some hope not only to ourselves but to the world.

It was the denial of pain that made possible the storm troopers in Germany.

It is the denial of pain that keeps apartheid alive in South Africa.

It is the denial of pain that could bring about the nuclear holocaust.

It is in the loss of the capacity to weep that humanity is lost.

We must not deny pain and the capacity to weep. We must not let the world lose contact with this power.

10

Tears, Power and Protest

It is the world's worst crime its babies grow dull ... limp and
leaden eyed.

Vachel Lindsay

Powerlessness and helplessness are among the most basic and
destructive human experiences. We all know these feelings and
depending on our previous history, health, or constitution they
can arouse terror, anger, apathy or the most damaging of the
defence mechanisms – denial. They can also arouse the will to
challenge fate. We are born with the urge to protest and the
potential for power. Life distorts that capacity, and forces us to
learn devious ways of expressing distress, or to bury it so deep that
we feel ourselves totally powerless. That direct protest is the
meaning of the child's first cry. It is a powerful message which
proclaims the child's sense of her right to exist, take up space and
be attended to. The world into which she has exploded is less
attractive than the one she was forced into leaving, and which no
matter how much she seeks, she will never regain. 'It's not fair', is
the passionate assertion that rings through childhood as soon as
words are put to feelings. 'It's not fair', has been the source of
powerful human movements for freedom, happiness and liberation. So what goes wrong? What sometimes happens in growing
up that turns some of us from creatures who battle to have our
needs met, who shout and scream with frustration if our existence
is denied, into apparently passive, disinterested adults, reluctant to
confront issues or use energy creatively?

Apart from those exhausted by the struggle before we even leave
the womb, each is born with a sense of what we need for survival.
We demand that the pain of hunger be eased. We demand that the
discomfort of our bodies be attended to. We demand to be held
and nurtured. Babies born without this capacity often die if they
have to cope with an infection or the trauma of surgical correction
to a congenital defect. Nurses and surgeons talk approvingly of

children who struggle to survive. 'She's a real fighter', they'll say. The baby who thrusts hungrily for its mother's nipple is applauded and enjoyed. But those babies are the lucky ones. Some are not applauded and enjoyed, their demands are not responded to, their needs are always subject to the convenience of the adults caring for them. They learn that they cannot influence or change their fate. When infant needs are met, promptly and lovingly, a sense of power is born. The cry of protest has been acknowledged, treated with respect and has produced results. The infant is sovereign in her own kingdom.

But this changes. To some extent it must change if new adults with some sense of cooperation and sharing, of delaying the immediate satisfactions of their bodies, are to be available for the tasks of the next generation. The child's sense of power is restricted as the wishes of adults to regain the pattern of their own lives make them resist meeting the anarchic, ruthless demands of the infant. Parents, but more often outsiders, say things like, 'You can't let a baby rule your life', or a husband will protest that his needs are ignored. Patterns of care are substituted for passionate caring and the child learns to adapt.

Timing is important. The happiest way through this dilemma, without a real solution, is for the child to exert power over its environment for as long as possible and then, as it grows in understanding and ability, for power to be shared between the child and adult carers. The simplest formula distinguishes between needs and wants . . . of both the child and the adults involved.

It is surprising in practice to find how seldom child and adult needs conflict if the adults reassess their needs. A woman may have thought she had a need to urinate or defecate in privacy. That is quickly reassessed as a want faced with a screaming baby who has a need to be held no matter what the mother is doing. There is frequently a conflict between child needs and adult wants and later, as the child grows, between child wants and adult wants.

The idea of sharing power with children is not always easy for adults to accept. Adults lose most. We have such strong conditioning that adult power must not be questioned, that sharing power with our children seems dangerous. The very idea of power is powerful and when we wrest it back from our parents we are reluctant to risk letting go again, particularly to our children. Perhaps the very idea reactivates the dangerous feeling we battened down when forced to accept our parents' power over us.

Parental advocates of power sharing have described positive results with even quite small children. One father who always faced his two-year-old's fury when he tried to wash his face, brush his hair or wipe his bottom resolved the conflict by offering the child the opportunity to do to his father whatever he was doing to him, namely wash his father's face, brush his father's hair, wipe his father's bottom. The result was magical, if more time-consuming. A young mother, tiring of breastfeeding after twenty months but meeting massive resistance to weaning from her child, agreed with the child that she would continue to breastfeed during the night but discontinue during the day. For the first few weeks after the agreement started the child demanded about ten opportunities to breastfeed during every night, then gradually gave up night-time feeding. In turn the mother was able to compromise and occasionally offer a breastfeed during the day, so both mother and child learned.

The daily lives of infants and young children often erode their initial feelings of power. They are picked up and put down; they are fed, often when it suits the adult rather than the child; they are bathed or changed at times bearing no relation to their needs. They are passed from one adult to another like parcels, without consultation; they are put to bed at times that suit the household rather than their needs to sleep. They are expected, if girls, to kiss, without making a fuss, any adult whom their parent wants to flatter; they are interrupted in activities which adults see as 'only playing' whenever the adult wants either their bodies in a different place or to clean the space occupied. If they explore the world they are frequently hauled back without explanation; interesting objects are torn from their grasp because they are either valuable or dangerous. Protest is regarded as rebellion and even normally reasonable parents turn purple with rage that their child is 'defying' them. I remember one woman friend whom I had always seen as sensible and reasonable, turning into a terrifying Medusa-like figure screaming at her lively, disobedient, three-year-old son, 'I'll break your spirit'. God only knows what demons from her own childhood were unlocked in that encounter.

Children cared for by substitute parents in nursery-type groups are even less likely to gain a share of power. There are seldom enough adults to cope with the varying demands and the energy of a group of small children. Most activities have to be carried out in routines and the 'good' children are seen as those who do not protest. Going to the lavatory becomes not an exciting opportunity to explore the marvellous mechanism and enjoyable sensations of one's body, but a mechanical trick completed as speedily as possible. So too with eating meals and putting on coats. Speed in response to demands and a passivity which allows you to be tugged and pulled and wiped when those in authority decide that's what's necessary, is virtuous.

With this emphasis on children doing as they are told, with messages that children have no power to question parental or indeed any adult decisions, it is not surprising that children do not protest when sexually abused. This is particularly true for girls. There may be some recognition of a boy's need for autonomy, for aggression even against a parent, although that must be muted, but girls are often doomed to powerlessness from the moment someone looks between their legs and sees no penis. Because that is how their sex is identified when born, not by the joyful recognition of female genitalia, but by the sex organs they haven't got.

At the next stage of their lives, going either to nursery school or to school proper, these lessons are reinforced. The ideal image is of the nice, polite child whose behaviour is always predictable, no tears, no tantrums, no fuss. This trains children for an urban adult world, constantly demanding obedience and conformity. Queue here for a train ticket, queue there for the train. Don't protest if you're pushed and shoved, don't protest if your boss shouts at you. Don't protest if made redundant, queue quietly for dole money. Don't protest if you become ill and don't protest waiting for hours in a hospital out-patient department.

As adults we face disasters over which we seem powerless – death, disease, disability, famine or earthquake. Others are socially determined ... poverty, bad housing or unemployment. But people's reactions vary widely. Some people go under in disaster, some people not only survive but triumph. Out of the disaster, they find a new serenity and capacity to help others. Even those who have in the past appeared totally defeated can surprise us with newfound strength. Some people not only face death or disaster with serenity, disability with courage and humour, poverty and unemployment with resolution, but add the determination to change and improve a society that brings such pain and injustice to its citizens. Why should this be?

Total acceptance of one's powerlessness is very rare. It usually leads to death. Holding on to some power to make decisions is necessary if we are to function at the simplest level. Those who appear passive frequently use techniques of manipulation or covert delinquency to keep some control over their lives. This is expressed in their jobs (if employed) and in their relationships. They can use their power in negative ways, by becoming hooked on drugs or alcohol and escaping the demands of ordinary living. Sadistic and violent killers are frequently people who have been offered no normal outlets for this human need to have a sense of power. Denis Nilson and Charles Manson are both examples.

The most destructive effects of powerlessness lie in the ordinary lives of men and women. An upbringing which insensitively limits their sense of power, inevitably limits their ability to own the power of their feelings. If their infant expressions of tears, anger and rage have consistently met with no positive response, it will be given up in exhaustion and replaced with hopeless whimpering. If their toddler tantrums are suppressed in ways that teach that not just the tantrum but the whole child is unacceptable, the capacity to disagree strongly will be damaged. But since our feelings, while they appear to emerge one at a time, are entangled under the surface like the roots of a tree, when one is rejected, the confidence to use any may be threatened. Expressions of loving or energetic feelings may be abandoned along with the expression of anger.

Those who crumble most severely under pressure may be those whose personal history as children is not only of their self-determination being consistently thwarted and defeated, but who saw their parents as equally powerless to help themselves or their children. This is why a sense of powerlessness is particularly destructive in communities devastated by unemployment or poverty. Any social worker or health visitor experiences seeing small children clustering fearfully behind their mother as she suspiciously answers the door, not knowing if the person knocking is a friend or an enemy. These children live in an atmosphere which lacks safety or confidence that the external world is one which they can control or influence. If school trips are arranged, the parents are powerless to find the money to pay for them. Opportunities for higher education for a bright child represent a threat to a fragile economy and are rejected. Where better-off children can persuade their mothers to buy them something, in poor families 'good' children learn not to ask.

But it is not only children of the poor who suffer from the

erosion of their power. Successful working-class and middle-class families have more choice in financial matters, and that is an important component of power, but they can so strangle their children's sense of power by rigid control that they inculcate fear. They build a box round their imaginations so that any ideas different from those of the parents are not allowed to penetrate. Christopher Wiseman's poem, *The Box*, says it.

> *his progressive*
> *behaviourist parents*
> *brought him up in a box*
> *until he was 18*
>
> *it worked well*
> *feeding and cleaning him*
> *giving illusions*
> *of day and night*
> *it was germ-free*
> *and kept at a constant*
> *temperature and humidity*
> *it had music piped in*
> *and books to read*
> *even carefully*
> *selected movies to watch*
>
> *when he was 18*
> *following the accidental*
> *death of his parents*
> *he was discovered*
> *and released*
> *and wandered out*
> *with amazement*
> *into the world*
>
> *two weeks later*
> *they found him*
> *in a deserted house*
> *frantically hammering*
> *together a long box*
> *with glass sides*

Identification with our parental oppressors has to be faced in childhood. To create us in their image our parents, or their substitutes, drive a bargain with us. 'Become what we want you to become and we will feed you, protect you, love you. Defy us and we will punish you and withdraw our love. There will be no compromise. Not only must you do what we want you to do but you must love us for making you do what you don't want to do. You must also believe that we are right to punish you'. And we do believe them.

Since no-one can ever be totally what their parents expect, in adult life when things go wrong it is easy to move back into a childlike feeling that it was our own fault and that we had failed to live up to the expectations of those in authority. Such people have no resources to fall back on and feel depressed and helpless. Nor are they equipped to resist oppression from those whom they should see as equals, school mates, colleagues or neighbours.

If at the same time, other voices reinforce those in our head – voices of social prejudice which say that, 'Anyone can get a job', or 'Women are stupid', 'Black people can't be trusted' or 'Everyone on the dole is a scrounger', our identification with the oppressor is complete. It is the right to protest, to question, to challenge that has been denied. The early cry of protest is smothered and not developed into curiosity, questioning and the ability to find alternative solutions to problems. If it survives at all, it shows in the corrupted form of attacks on those even weaker than ourselves.

Middle-class children and particularly upper-middle-class children have a decided advantage. They may have had to mute their protests in infancy and early childhood, but in adult life their environment allows many more opportunities for intellectual deviancy, creativity and eccentricity. Edith Sitwell in her autobiography describes the desperate pain of her childhood with governesses trying to fit her into a mould acceptable to her parents, physically as well as mentally. She was strapped into a harness to improve her posture. But the richness of her environment and the choices available in adult life provided some compensation.

The capacity to protest openly only survives if it brings results. It is helped by seeing that the adults around you have power. The need for power in our lives is so strong that it dies very slowly in spite of the slow accumulation of eroding experiences. Each step in the loss of power is an experience of distress, an accumulation of hurts. That results in apathy and acceptance of further humiliations. It is the fear of reactivating hurt and humiliation that makes adults shrug their shoulders and say things like, 'You can't beat the system', 'Life's simpler if you just do what you're told', or 'What can I do', without wanting an answer. The anger which would be the normal response to rejection, along with shouts of protest and tears of frustration has been buried, unable to survive being ignored.

It is in the interests of those with power that it is kept in a small number of hands. We have seen how much easier life is for the parents of powerless, unprotesting children. Life is also easier for teachers who have unprotesting pupils, jailors who have unprotesting prisoners, employers with an unprotesting workforce. Many men prefer powerless women in homes and offices. Our knowledge about the sexual abuse of children only makes sense if we recognize the power of men and the trained powerlessness of the children whose bodies they use. Residential care for people who are elderly is too often a battleground in which the struggle of residents to retain some power over their lives conflicts with the needs of staff to run a 'tidy' and trouble-free establishment. When we talk about power and powerlessness we are too often talking about the oppressor and the oppressed.

Any society which contains a large number of powerless people is not a healthy society. A society which tries to keep the lid on protest and the human need for autonomy relies for stability on people being apathetic and without the energy to make changes. The fewer powerless people, the healthier a society. It may not be calm or static, but it will have vigour and the capacity to question directions and values. How does our society match up to the ideal of a society where as many members as possible have access to their own power? How can we make power available to more people?

FIGHTING AGAINST POWERLESSNESS

He who has a why to live for can bear almost any how.

Nietzsche

If we try to understand how we can move from apathy to creativity, or from spiritual death to life, we can look at some of the ways in which people have succeeded. The average human being, no matter her apparent powerlessness, finds ways of fighting against helplessness. She knows that if she yields, apathy and death will follow. This is clearly recorded in the history of prisoners of the Nazi concentration camps. I don't use the word victims, because the word signifies helplessness. The survivors of the camps did not see themselves as victims; often those who did, died.

But others describe how they found different ways to hold on to a sense of power. Many studies show that it is prisoners with a strong faith in the purpose of their lives who survived best. These were particularly political and religious prisoners in countries like Russia both before and after the revolution, today in South America and in South Africa. Political prisoners believe their imprisonment has some meaning, that they are part of an international struggle and have behind them not only the power of, perhaps millions of political comrades in the outside world, but of world history. The religious prisoners believe that God himself is with them and some powerful and moving testimonies have come from prisoners, struggling with the idea that God had abandoned them, then finding renewed faith and meaning.

As powerful in a quite different way are the techniques used by people who had no political or religious faith which they could use to bolster the assaulted sense of their own power. One friend of mine, brought up by her father in a way which encouraged her to have a sense of power, held on to this in spite of the terrible experiences of being separated from her family in a concentration camp, in spite of being stripped and shaved, in spite of hardships and humiliations. She held on to the sense he had given her of her 'specialness', even though this drove other inmates to nickname her 'The Duchess'. It became important to feel she had some power over her captors, that she was not always the subject of their decisions. One technique to achieve this was not to eat her bread ration at once but to divide it and eat the second half when *she* chose to, not when the authorities decided. In doing this and giving it significance, she also developed a sense of superiority, even of contempt, for the women who gobbled theirs down the moment it was handed out. This sense of being 'special' was obviously an important factor in her survival, and contains a message for all parents who wish to give their children survival strengths.

Hope and anger can be equally therapeutic. In the Second World

War, a new inmate to a prisoner-of-war camp in Italy found his compatriots, from a proud English regiment, lying in their urine and faeces, convinced the Allies had lost. Still fresh and with confidence in the future, he shouted and screamed, calling them cowards and scum until he aroused enough anger to start the slow processes of cleaning up their hut.

If a situation is too dangerous, as in the concentration camps, or as it can be in a prison or some mental hospitals, to risk anger being shown, covert anger is mobilized in the form of delinquency and various forms of trickery. Some delinquency can be destructive, used randomly as much against fellow inmates as against staff, but even that serves to keeping the energy of anger alive, bubbling on the back burner. Trickery can be more creative, as when camp prisoners trapped the lice from the bodies of the corpses who had died of typhus and inserted them into the newly-laundered shirt collars of the SS officers.

The western industrialized world grievously underestimates the power of this survival technique. Pagan cultures have always incorporated some such legitimizing figure like Puck who pricked pomposity. The North American Indian cultures brought this to a high art in the figure of the Trickster who features in many of their myths. It offers a fascinating mixture of covert anger and humour.

This combination is the source of satire, caricature and cartoon; it can be a powerful political weapon as in both Hungary and Czeckoslovakia, and in the satirical magazine *Crokodil*. In a less dramatic but very effective way the satirical television programme of the 1960s *That Was the Week, That Was*, played a part in the downfall of a Conservative government. These capacities grow out of the humorous acceptance by parents that children will continually try to evade accepting authority. If the parents do not see that as a hanging matter; if they, while staying firm, acknowledge the skills exerted in, for example, avoiding bed times, a child learns to value her capacity for creative challenge.

Using the experience of survivors, it is possible to build a catalogue of capacities which enable personal power to be maintained and helplessness avoided even in intolerable situations. These include a sense of humour, curiosity, an awareness of injustice, faith in the future and the feeling of being a lucky, i.e., special person. The most destructive loss is loss of faith in the future. In the camps, the prisoners who smoked rather than exchanged the cigarettes they had earned for food from the guards, were seen by their friends as doomed. They were exchanging their lives for a temporary pleasure. As Camus said, 'A man devoid of hope and conscious of being so has ceased to belong to the future'.

Frankl describes how one prisoner had a dream that the war would be over on 30 March 1945. When the date passed without good news, he died. People who lose faith in the future give up and slide into apathy, which in the camps inevitably led to death. Nurses describe how the same thing happens in hospitals, and therapists in the alternative health movement know that their primary task with many illnesses, particularly cancer, is to offer hope which they believe can mobilize the body's defences. People growing old, slowly becoming imprisoned in the 'camp' of a failing body, who constantly plan for the future, a holiday or a grandchild's birthday have a better life expectation than those who sit and wait for death.

Central to all survival and creativity is the retention of the capacity to feel and express that feeling. There is a difference between powerlessness and helplessness. We can be powerless and not feel helpless, we can be helpless but not feel powerless. Those who have no passionate political or religious conviction which can give meaning to suffering, rely on the conviction that life has meaning for its own sake, that to exist has value and is an experience to be cherished and developed in all circumstances. This was what Dostoevski meant when he said that the only thing he dreaded was not to be worthy of his suffering. But this is a very demanding view. It implies that the only meaning of life is the one we give it.

But to believe in one's own value as distinct from a belief in history or in a God who gives one value, means constantly having to live with vulnerability, with one's pain and confusion. It means keeping alive, almost without a frame of reference, not only the curiosity, the humour and the anger, but also the capacity for horror, for disgust, for indignation and a sense of injustice. To retain the ability to feel insulted is important whether we are in a concentration camp, a home for elderly people or the out-patient department of a hospital.

These are fragile capacities, perhaps developing late in the evolutionary scale since our more complex societies create so many threats to self-esteem. We should make it easier for fellow citizens both to be protected from damaging experiences but also to resist and change them when they happen. We can do this in two ways.

The first is to encourage and applaud those who bring from their early experience those creative survival qualities we have identified. We all have a right to laugh at authority, to feel angry if insulted, to be horrified at cruelty to ourselves and others, indignant at injustice and to weep for pain. It becomes possible for that anger, indignation and sorrow to be translated into thoughtful ways of overcoming their causes. We have to celebrate in our daily lives the capacity to show feeling and we can help young parents to respect their children's capacity to do the same.

We need also to find ways of helping people whose capacities have been blocked or distorted, so that instead of 'taking arms against a sea of troubles and by opposing end them', they relapse into passivity, identify with their oppressors and blame themselves. Some of the degrading treatment we mete out to our citizens who are growing old is only possible because they have lost their capacity to feel insulted and to protest. Their sense of their own value has melted in helplessness and powerlessness. The awkward, difficult old people who continue to care about justice for themselves and the people around them, like the concentration camp prisoners who held on to the same feeling, also have a better chance of living longer. The core of caring about other people has to be caring for oneself. That for some people is difficult. Many can feel pain and outrage for others; we must also be able to feel it for ourselves. Unable to care for ourselves, unable to feel our own pain, we are unable to care for anyone else, unable to feel anyone else's pain. This is the ultimate damage of an uncared-for childhood.

Those who took that path were the people who ran the concentration camps, those with the 'stony tearless faces'. But we should remember that every camp survivor can tell a story of one or more guards who tried on occasion to be helpful, individuals who had kept alive some capacity to be moved by human distress. Many could only do their jobs with the aid of alcoholic anaesthesia – always a sign that someone is in a painful situation. The gas chamber and crematoria attendants were kept constantly supplied with schnapps.

It is in early childhood that we first learn if we have the right to protest against pain and injustice. If that was not wholly denied us – and to have it fully denied us is rare – if we secured even a modest acceptance of our feelings, we can be given a second chance. We can be lucky and have a grannie or grandad who gives us bits of loving and with that keep alive our energy and courage. We can have a social worker or a teacher who treats us as if we were a bit special and reinforces tiny bits of self-esteem. We may find someone who can see past our defences and loves, nurtures and heals the hurt bits. We may find through a child of our own the opportunity to break into the cycle of deadness of feeling and offer some of what we would have wanted for ourselves. We may, in a variety of ways, find the core of our pain, transform our use of it and find hope.

We can take our pain out into the world and ask those who also suffer to join us in transforming it. The very act of sharing pain, of weeping together, can bring a shift of energy.

It is not possible to move directly from apathy to creativity. There is a series of steps on the path that have to be worked through. If one is blocked, if opportunities to express feelings are denied, then the person involved immediately retreats to an earlier position. The feeling and the behaviour associated with it does not go away. Following the advice of Camus, that then becomes the task, 'to root ourselves in the solid earth of our distress'. We can look at our emotional life as lying on a spectrum of energy which runs between spiritual death and life. At the lowest point above total non-functioning, we can sink into apathy. At our highest point of living we are in touch with creativity. The steps that lie between these points are familiar to all. Each step is more alive and healthier than the one before.

Each of us started life ready to be creative and cooperative. It was the experience into which we were born that determined if we stayed in that state or if we were pushed down the scale of response, our capacities crippled, our energies drained or thwarted. For some the diminishment of our capacities came in infancy, for some as toddlers, for others it was the experience of school and insensitive authority.

Some of us, but too few, have been lucky. This last group seem to hold their power within themselves. They have less need to react to the approval or disapproval of other people. They are interested in other people but not dependent on them. They have the capacity to experience great happiness and to be in touch with a wide range of feelings.

Those of us who have not been so lucky find ourselves struggling usually in the middle range, with occasional experiences of the joy of cooperation or creativity, and occasional experiences of a

THE PATH TO LIFE

APATHY or MEANINGLESSNESS
↓
DESPAIR
↓
HELPLESSNESS or POWERLESSNESS
↓
DEPRESSION
↓
COVERT PROTEST
↓
IRRITATION or DELINQUENCY
↓
OPEN PROTEST
↓
COOPERATION
↓
CREATIVITY

sense of apathy or meaninglessness. We are sensitive to other people's opinion of us and easily pushed down the spectrum of feeling when we meet rejection or disapproval. Some get stuck for shorter or longer periods of time in the areas of apathy, helplessness, powerlessness and covert anger and irritability. Moving from these to open protest, cooperation and creativity is one step at a time and at each stage the person's position needs to be acknowledged, accepted and respected by someone else before they can move up that spectrum. At each stage we have to be given a modicum of hope that the journey is worth making before risking making a move. The crucial point comes in the move from covert to open protest. Will the world allow us to express anger and sorrow? If that right was denied to us in the tears of our infancy and childhood, will we be given a second chance by the people with whom we now live? Each is meaningless without the other: the sorrow of depression holds glowing anger at its heart, the blaze of anger covers the pain of tears. Irritation and delinquency are simply ways of distracting us from unremitting pain.

THE PATH TO SPIRITUAL DEATH

CREATIVITY
↓
COOPERATION
↓
OPEN PROTEST OR IRRITATION
↓
COVERT PROTEST
↓
DEPRESSION
↓
POWERLESSNESS OR HELPLESSNESS
↓
DESPAIR
↓
APATHY OR MEANINGLESSNESS

Wherever people come together to share problems and help each other, this pattern is seen. All groups where people take action to deal with problems in their own communities will be familiar with the process. Members of the group join at different stages in their personal emotional journey. They may have been dragged reluctantly to a meeting by a friend, but unless they had a spark of hope they wouldn't have gone at all. They may continue to go, express a sense of helplessness which if it is acknowledged and respected will help them move on to a grieving for their own sadness, taking the form of depression and, with luck, tears to bring relief. Tears linked to depression are always an encouraging sign that there is energy. At a later stage it becomes the energy of our anger. If the person's depression and tears are also respected and supported by the group without the need for them to rush off to a doctor and get tranquillizers which will suppress the grieving and pitch them back into helplessness, they emerge to a tiny gleam of hope.

But hope is dangerous, it can be betrayed. The next stage of growing energy is the testing-out by covert anger of that energy. Covert anger is anger seen as dangerous, which cannot be openly expressed and has to be acted out. There are many opportunities. Social work customers have skilled techniques. They will not turn up for appointments or, if they do come, they sit and say nothing.

One young man, after sitting for weeks and saying nothing began leaving behind him rough, ungrammatical but mercilessly vivid letters in which he expressed anger, contempt and disgust against me, the service and in letter after letter against his parents, his school and his whole life. I accepted these with humility in the face of their terrible and powerful feeling. One day, as I was trying to convey respect for his capacity to have survived the awfulness, his hostile silence melted into tears. We wept together. Life never became perfect for him, but he moved into a fairly stable balance between open protest and cooperation. He was lucky to find a wife with whom he could express his sorrow and anger in tears and words but, most important, with his own children he broke the pattern of oppression in which he had been reared.

The leap from covert to open protest can be frightening. We need to have confidence that our feelings as well as our words will be heard. The ability to protest openly is always linked with hope. This is true at a communal as well as a personal level. The more hierarchical and authoritarian an institution, the greater the level of covert protest, delinquency and irritability among the staff and customers. The same thing happens in whole countries. In Eastern Europe we saw how open protest and hope are linked. The less hope, the less protest; the more hope, the greater the protest. The more totalitarian the society, the higher the level of covert process; the more democratic the society, the more open the protest. The more open the protest, the more realistic and less paranoid it is likely to be. Paranoia flourishes where protest is suppressed.

In the intervening stage, before open protest is fully achieved, there may be uncertainty about how to respond. Flashes of creativity are shown, humour and trickery being evoked to challenge authority. In public demonstrations, local residents, groups of parents, peace protesters or trades unionists will write witty slogans on banners, make and burn effigies. More dramatically, in the forties and fifties bags of rats might be thrown across the counter of Glasgow's housing department. In Manchester, more recently, bags of cockroaches have been thrown at officials. If these messages can be heard and responded to, not with blind anger but taken seriously, cooperation between the two sides to the dispute becomes possible.

It is when hope is thwarted that anger becomes destructive. We see this in rioting in areas of deprivation, which when put down hard by the police drives the community back into covert anger, usually in the form of delinquency which damages fellow citizens. Many simply return to apathy, a state which suits the holders of power.

Individuals, groups and communities have at some time to take responsibility themselves for converting their covert or destructive energy to open, creative protest. Some exceptional people can do this on their own, but most need support from others. A belief in a god, a belief in an idea, or the conviction that we gain dignity from the love of another human being are the most common sources from which we draw strength. In communities, sharing the struggle is all-important. Recognizing that we are not alone in our suffering gives dignity, sharing our tears validates them and gives the right to protest. As individuals and in groups we recover the right to state our view of the world, a right that was taken away from us as children. We regain the ability to deal with authority figures without fearing that we will be made fools of; we can express what we think and feel without fear of being made to feel ashamed; we can practice protest against cruelty and injustice without embarrassment.

Individuals, groups and governments do not normally oppress us by dramatic threats against life and freedom. They use a seemingly more fragile web which first winds round us in childhood. It is a web of shame, embarrassment and uneasy guilt which controls us as surely as it did our parents. It's a web that discourages curiosity and protest. It's a web that encourages people to take the easy way out rather than to confront issues head on. It holds us in ways that leave decisions to others, persuades us to respect authority without questioning its provenance. It chokes us if we seek to explore feelings that lie behind the face we learn to turn to the world. It inhibits the energy that makes us want to change the world and makes us say, 'What's the point, nothing I do will make any difference'.

By understanding these patterns of restriction and ways of overcoming them we can enable ourselves, other individuals, groups and communities to claim a fair share of power. In a world which increasingly emphasizes conformity in all but the most trivial issues, the preservation and nurturance of creative protest is crucial for all our futures.

11

Conclusions

You are either your own saviour or your own worst enemy.
                                        The Dalai Lama, quoting the Buddha

I want to finish this book by repeating the themes I have written about. We have looked at the way in which as children we learn how to deal with our pain, grief and sorrow, our frustration and anger. We have looked at the ways in which as adults our loves and our hatreds with other adults are shaped and influenced by our experiences. We have looked at the way big organizations like hospitals, departments of social security, housing departments and prisons make it impossible for us to tell how we really feel.

We have also seen how our gender, whether we are male or female, too often is allowed to decide what feelings we are permitted; and how our parents' own experience of being allowed to cry, or not, has influenced the freedom, or lack of it, which they have offered us to express our feelings through tears.

Above all, we have seen how our emotional and physical health is closely linked to the way we feel, and how tears can both help us understand and help release damaging tension: that if we can stay in touch with our feelings of pain we can convert and use them creatively in the world. Our feelings, our emotions are responses to the day-to-day events of life, part of the price we pay for the extraordinary experience and privilege of being a human being. We have a more complex and therefore potentially a more reward-ing relationship with the world than any fellow-creature on the planet. We are the only ones who can clarify and demonstrate distress to fellow humans, not only those we personally know but – through books, newspapers and television – others all over the world. We alone can take that distress and convert it into energy and action. Some use distress to power destructiveness, but we all have the capacity to use it creatively. Pain and distress can be displaced by human beings into forms of torturing and damaging their fellow humans, or can be acknowledged, brought into the open and used to nurture all forms of creativity.

184

The gift we carry within which enables us to acknowledge and learn to use our grief and our pain, is our capacity to weep. We do not have to learn to weep, the gift comes with life itself. We have had to learn *not* to weep. Many of us, if we want to rediscover our humanity, have to relearn weeping. To do that is not always easy but it is important, not only for us as individuals but for the whole society of which we are a part.

The path is not always easy. Clement of Alexandria described a similar journey. 'We may not be taken up and transported to our journey's end, but must travel thither on foot, traversing the whole distance of the narrow way'. We have to learn first to weep for ourselves. Only then will we find ourselves able to weep with integrity for others, other human beings, other creatures on the planet and then for the planet itself. We start when we make contact with the broken and damaged parts of ourselves. Only then can we acknowledge the broken and damaged parts of other creatures and the world. Through our tears we can bring together the hurt parts of ourselves, and in finding our own healing share in the healing of others.

This century, more than any other in human history, has brought us a terrifying awareness of the dark and evil capacities of human nature. It is not that people in the past did not behave in evil and destructive ways; we have always known that human beings could be wicked and cruel. But in this century we have seen horrors. The Turks killed two million Armenians; the Germans killed six million Jews and an unknown number of Poles and other nationals apart from gypsies, the mentally ill, people with severe learning difficulties, and others physically disabled. The Russians killed fifteen million of their own people. The Americans napalmed Vietnamese villages.

All that was not very different in quality from the most horrifying experiences of the Middle Ages: the Inquisition; the burning of witches; the rape and destruction of towns by soldiers. It is not essentially different from the genocide of the north American Indians, the Maoris and the Aboriginal peoples, the massacre by the British troops at Amritsar.

Modern technology like gas chambers and napalm added to the horror by increasing efficiency but that was not the significant difference. What horrified us most was that we had the illusion in Europe, fed by the new scientific age of the Victorians, that we were becoming better people. Good drains would give us not only healthy bodies but healthy minds. In the public schools cold baths and exercise would drive out the demons of evil thoughts. As we learned about evolution, we believed that we were evolving into more sensible, more rational people. We believed that with education came good sense, with learning and culture, love of painting and music, came emotional sensibility and decency.

It has been the realization that rationality and reason have failed that shocked us. All human wickedness needs to have agents who deny the importance of feeling. To shovel people into the gas chambers, for troops in Vietnam or China to shoot down villagers or students, it is necessary not to be moved by tears of protest. If you evict people from their homes in order to build a new dam, you need to deny the importance of their tears. In London, to walk past men and women sleeping in boxes you need to deny their tears. To accept poverty and homelessness for women and their small children, to accept the daily humiliations and injustice we inflict on the unemployed, the physically and emotionally disadvantaged in our society, you need to deny their tears ... and always to deny your own.

To build a new motorway you have to think it doesn't matter to destroy the habitat of wild birds and animals and cause distress; in order to burn down trees you have not to care about the delicate ecostructure of the planet and how we may damage that. In the name of progress, we have given power to people who take pleasure in not caring about people's tears, and who continue to rationalize what they do in the name of progress and profit.

This is the politics of tears.

In order to get people to behave like this it is necessary to tell them that tears are stupid, tears are childish, tears are a sign of weakness, important people don't cry, clever people don't cry. Of course women cry but that just shows how weak – how womanly – it is to cry.

I have written about women and how they hold on to the capacity to weep. Yet we seldom see women using that capacity to weep and to retain contact with their feelings taking the lead in protest about public pain. They use their capacities almost exclusively to express feelings about relationships, with lovers, with husbands, with children.

Some weeping that takes place seems a waste of time and energy. It appears to give importance to events which are not always worthy of all that passion. The causes of the tears often trivialize that very important function. Women, if they gave more dignity to themselves, would not, so often, let themselves be victims. As I was writing this I had a visit from a young, beautiful, weeping woman. Behind a veil of bright hair she was hiding a savage bruise, and she showed me her ribs where she had been kicked. The man who had done this was emotionally inhibited, unable to deal with his own pain and determined to make her suffer to ease it for him. By now even her capacity for duty, tenderness and conviction that she is responsible for his happiness is wearing thin. My hope is that her need for love, unmet in early childhood, will not lead her into a similar trap with the next partner who appears to offer it to her. If she does not use her tears to grow, if she simply continues to weep helplessly without mobilizing intelligence and capacity for action, that will happen.

But it is important that, even if for the wrong reasons, women retain the capacity to weep and teach men to do the same. Most have managed to avoid the sterile traps of cynicism, of denial, of detachment and the world needs their emotional freedom. What matters is not that we weep but what happens when the weeping stops.

The force that lies behind our tears, our pain, is a powerful source of energy. We know if unmobilized it turns into physical pain, tension and illness at an individual level. If we do not turn it against ourselves, we can turn it against others. We can hurt people because they remind us of the pain we suffered at the hands of our mothers, we can humiliate our partners because our fathers never gave us dignity, we can abuse our children as we were abused. That is all terrible, that private incestuous damage that goes on in families. But it is also played out on a wider screen. In group action the pain can be transformed into a powerful agent of action, also destructive. We can riot and burn, we can explode bombs which kill indiscriminately.

On the other hand, the energy behind those tears, that pain, can be used creatively. It underlies the determination that life should be better for our children than it was for us, it can evoke the tenderness that compels us to ease pain and distress that our children may experience. Perhaps more importantly, it can fuel the tenderness which is aroused by the needs of strangers. It is this energy that has created the great humanitarian movements of the world. We passionately need to mobilize that energy in the world in which we live to-day.

HOW DO WE MOBILIZE THE ENERGY?

Don't fear tears – the tears of others, especially those of children.
Respect tears.
Listen to what our own tears are saying.
Listen to what other people's tears are saying.
Look at people who are crying tears.
Look at people who are crying silently.
Read faces.
Hear the sorrows that lie behind words.
Honour distress.
Respect pain, both physical and emotional, in yourself and others.
Share your pain with others.
Share your tears with others.
Be cautious about tranquillizers and anti-depressants.
Be cautious with any drugs, including alcohol, that anaesthetize emotional pain.
Be cautious with any behaviour, getting your own back, gambling or falling in love again, that anaesthetizes emotional pain.
Grieve for your pain with your whole heart, then let it go.
If the wound is one which will never heal, and there are some, don't try to cover up and deny it. Acknowledge it as part of your life to which you give respect and appropriate attention.

HAVING MOBILIZED THE ENERGY, WHAT DO WE DO WITH IT?

There are some very private pains, like the death of someone we love, but even these private pains may have roots in the way our society is organized. We are not solitary creatures. Each has automatic membership of the human group, and many pains we experience have sources which are not private but very public. The death of the person we love may have been caused because the safety regulations at their place of work had not been put into practice. That may have been caused by lack of proper supervision by the factory inspectors, and that may have been due to government cuts which left the department responsible short-staffed. The humiliations and injustice, the poverty, the exclusion and the destructiveness which are the sources of pain and distress to so many of us who live on this planet are no accident. They are the product of human decision-making powered by insensitivity, and often by greed. When the weeping stops, these are issues which must be tackled.

Retaining the tenderness, the sensitivity and contact with our own pain enables us to ally ourselves with others. But the expression of distress is not enough, any more than it is for a child. Action must follow to relieve that distress. But we have no mothers any more, nor fathers, to relieve our distress: nor should we ask for them because we are no longer children. Seeking for leaders to take the place of our parents reinforces our helplessness, impedes us rather than taking us forward to new and more mature ways of living together. We have to be our own mothers and fathers and take thought about how we can relieve our communal distress. It is we who have to translate that thought into action because without action nothing changes.

Those who are privileged in any society, who hold power, do not give it up lightly. They resist with every weapon, both physical and psychological, at their command. One most powerful psychological weapon is that feelings must always be suppressed in favour of reason. Those who want that power shared must raise a banner where feelings and reason are linked. The bridge that links them is the gift of our tears.

Epilogue

Life must be lived forwards, but it can only be understood
backwards.

Soren Kierkegaard.

On a scorchingly hot July day, two years after my visit to the Hong
Kong refugee camp, a taxi set me down at a small Zen Buddhist
temple on the outskirts of a village deep in the Japanese countryside. The taxi driver asked if he would call later in the day to pick
me up. When I explained that I was staying for a week, he looked
incredulous and swept away muttering incomprehensibly.

Invited to Japan to speak at a social work conference, I had
decided to use the opportunity to explore one of the Japanese
'quiet' therapies described by Dr D. K. Reynolds, an American
therapist. I chose Naikan – from *nai* (inner) and *kan* (observation) –
because it was possible to do a concentrated course for one week. I
had no clear idea what would be involved.

The courtesy and love with which I was met by the Abbot of the
temple, the Reverend Usami, his wife and family and the monks,
overwhelmed me. The Japanese flag and the Union Jack were
entwined over the door and an interpreter had been invited to
attend our initial meeting since I had no Japanese and no one in the
temple spoke more than a few words of English. Within ten
minutes of arriving I realized that I must abandon myself to this
experience, shed all expectations and drift like a leaf on the wind,
opening myself to whatever came.

Within the next hour I was installed behind folding screens in a
corner of the small, beautiful temple, sitting cross-legged on a
cushion, facing a blank screen, with a dawning awareness of the
strict spiritual discipline surrounding me. This place in which my
life would be concentrated for fourteen hours a day for the next
week was called the *hoza*, a term used in Buddhism to describe a
place where the Buddha, or God if one believes in God, would
surround and see me. It was a private place for me, and the Naikan
which I was going to experience would also be private. I need only
share with the monks who would care for me, what I wished to
share.

My guide or *sensei* who settled me in had prepared a translation of the first questions I had to consider. I read that I had to examine myself in relationship to my mother from the time I was born until I was six years of age. I had to contemplate what I had received from her, what I had given her and ways in which I had troubled her. This seemed a simple task. What memories I had of those years were vividly clear.

Crying had not been allowed. 'What have you got to cry about?', she would shout at me. '*I* am the one who has suffered'. I suppose there was a time when I cried freely, not only with a sense of self-disgust. Perhaps when I was born, torn so roughly from my mother that the incision made by the surgeons to enable my father to penetrate her was torn more deeply into her flesh. I am sure she cried in rage and pain, and perhaps that first Sunday morning we sang a duet as I too cried in rage and pain. I never discovered the source of her rage, but I was often made to feel that I was the source of her pain.

She was twenty-three when I was born, and if the photographs tell the truth, as beautiful as a pre-Raphaelite painting. It was the colouring, my aunts who feared and envied her told me – the pale skin, the great mass of crinkly Titian hair, the sapphire blue eyes. They blamed that hair for her temper, those flashes of rage that left them stunned and shaken and were to do the same for me. They were afraid of her: I learned to be afraid *for* her.

She wanted me to be perfect – that's normal isn't it? Or is it? Before I was born, she told me, she used to walk in Glasgow's Queen's Park, thinking beautiful thoughts so that I would be beautiful. Later she told me that she didn't like the park because there were too many Jewesses there. But that may have been hindsight after she learned that Mussolini made the trains run on time and had drained the swamps. She was quick to learn the phrases that would impress. But if she did think about the Jewish women as I bobbed about in her womb, it may explain why I was not coppery beautiful like her but dark and sallow, with a weakness for Jewish men.

My tears seemed to be a threat – dangerous. Perhaps they truly were in ways I do not understand. I only know my father's response to me through the distorted lens of my mother's stories. It may have been that he, whom she loved with a bizarre obsessional hatred, would flee from my sounds of distress as he fled from hers. So, to keep me quiet, she stuffed her nipple into my mouth until I gagged. She was still trying to get me to suck when I was six. She told me it was because she loved me, but I was an evil child who doubted that.

I knew I was an evil child long before. Small, solemn and dark, by the time I was four and sent away to a convent school, I had given up hope. I had lost my father. I had lost my mother too when she left me with my grandmother whom I learned to love but now had also lost; now I had no one. I had known something was going to happen. For weeks my mother had trailed me round a succession of large buildings asking if they would keep me and explaining that she was unable to look after me. I don't remember the words but I remember the atmosphere. I remember my grandmother's helpless anger.

Suddenly her problem was solved and in a state of euphoria I was showered with new clothes – a navy nap coat, a black velour hat, gym tunic, blouses, underwear, long black woollen stockings. For the first time I saw the Liberty vests with which I was later to become so familiar as exercises for my paralysed fingers to button up. I didn't cry when I was left at the convent. Instead I wet the bed. Every night my body wept at the wrong end.

Neither did I cry during or after the only visit from my mother that I remember. I didn't do anything. We met in the convent parlour, a large stiff room with a waxed floor, plaster images of the Virgin Mary, St Theresa of Lisieux and paintings of saints in various poses of ecstacy. She was sitting on a hard chair when I was brought in to the room by a nun, and even my mother's capacity for dramatizing and sentimentalizing situations when she had an audience must have been defeated when she was presented with the small wooden creature I had become. For the first time the power was mine, not hers. The nun withdrew to leave us alone together but I would not let my mother near me. We were each alone and not together. It was the beginning of the end of my childhood. The final end of my childhood came two years later when, at the age of six, I left the convent on a stretcher suffering from infantile paralysis.

In the interval, as I waited for my fate to come and meet me, I learned to sew a fine seam (ten hemming stitches to the inch), I learned to read, and I learned that I was different from other children. They each had a father as well as a mother and none of them, apart from me, wet the bed. Every morning I wakened to find my nightdress soaked from hem to shoulders. The nun in charge of the dormitory, Mother Stanislaus, scolded, mocked, derided me, threatened me with the cane ... all to no avail. I continued to wet the bed every night.

Finally I was given the ultimate sanction. One morning on wakening, I was not allowed to dress. While the other girls were washing at the basins from where in the distance you could see the Ailsa Craig out in the Irish sea, I had to sit on my bed. Then, when all were ready and the crocodile formed to walk from the dormitory through the school to the refectory, the cold, smelly, wet sheet was stripped from my bed, wrapped round me and I was made to walk carrying it, by myself, at the very end of the line, followed only by Mother Stanislaus. Once in the refectory, I was paraded around, then made to sit by myself and wait until everyone had eaten before being marched back, by myself, to the dormitory to wash and dress before going to the schoolroom. That night, as I slept, I wet the bed again. It was my second awareness of power.

Now, sitting in the *hoza*, as I meditated on these first six years of my life, I felt myself flooded with bitterness. Perhaps here in this strange country, among people with whom I had no connections of any kind, I could, without feeling guilty, express my sense of having been betrayed from infancy. Perhaps too I could let go my painfully-acquired skills of trying to make sense of everything, which made it impossible for me to blame anyone for anything.

With the aid of the dictionary I prepared my responses carefully. What had I received from my mother? I slowly and ruthlessly listed ... anxiety, misery, loneliness, fear, grief, rage. It went on and on. What had I given her? Someone to love of course, it was obvious. But also a focus for her tempers and her dramas. Had I troubled her? I didn't think so. I had always been a good, obedient, submissive child.

When my *sensei* returned, I was ready, smiling. We each performed the ritual greeting of mutual respect, and I began. But before the first sentence was finished, he stopped me. 'This word', he said, '*anxiety*, what does it mean'? I was halted in mid-flight and turned to the dictionary. He checked the translation I offered in his and then shook his head. 'Naikan', he said, 'is not abstract. It is concrete. Let us take the first three years.' He bowed ceremoniously and left me with my little house of cards demolished.

When he returned two hours later, I had prepared a list of concrete words which I saw as utterly boring and irrelevant to my condition. I would, however, see this odd experience through. What had my mother given me? Food, warmth, clothes, shelter.

What had I given her? Nothing of course, how could I? What
trouble had I caused her? None really. Certainly I had been ill
frequently, but most children get ill.

My list was accepted and we moved on to the next three years
over the next two hours, and then again the next three years over
the next two hours. For the next two days, interrupted only by
meals, the temple prayers and a highly formal and ritualized
interview with the abbot, my life focussed on those three questions. 'What had my mother given me? What had I returned to her
and what trouble had I caused her?' I could vaguely discern that
there were other people in hidden corners of the temple but the
strict rules that I must not talk to anyone nor get up and walk
around without a specific purpose kept them as shadowy figures
from whom I heard only an occasional moan or the sound of
weeping.

By the end of my second day in the Temple my house of cards
had not only collapsed in ruins; it was torn into tiny useless scraps.
Gradually my perception of the world was shifting. Instead of
seeing *my* self and *my* needs as the fulcrum of all meaning, I was
beginning to build up a new picture of this twenty-three year old
girl who had given birth to me. Under-educated (she had left
school at eleven) beautiful, courageous, ambitious, she went
through her life trapped in an emotional and self-destructive
nightmare constantly running inside her head.

For the first time in my life I began to weep for her and her pain. I
saw her life as central, rather than mine. I was no longer the
misunderstood heroine of the most important story in the universe. I wept for twenty-four hours and intermittently for the
following two days. Before long I was weeping for myself as well,
for the pain of our joint lives, for the pain of existence and for her
husband and my father, whom I had hardly known and whose
time and place of death are still unknown to me. I had the most
extraordinary feeling as if the inside of my head had tilted so that I
saw the whole of my life from a different angle of vision.

That has never altered. I finally separated myself out from my
parents. I went through the same Naikan process for my father
that I had done for my mother, and subsequently with all the other
significant people in my life. When we are hurt by someone we
love it is as if we are caught on barbed wire. Each movement to
release ourselves causes greater and deeper pain as we make new
wounds, reactivate those unhealed and reopen old scars. Naikan

helped me to stop struggling and to see the unrepayable debt I owe both my parents for their gift to me of my life, no matter what happened after that. Somehow the barbed wire has dissolved.

Seven days after my arrival I left the Temple feeling as if the inside of my head had been taken out, washed, rinsed and dried, and put back sparklingly clean. The world looked as if it too had been washed clean. In the days after my weeping I had found myself overwhelmed with indescribable feelings of joy and love. It was as if I was on the borders of another country, another way of living. I try to hold on to those memories and sometimes when I'm alone, I am brushed by the same experience. I have learned to weep more easily with friends for joint pain but for my own I still seek privacy. The difference is that now I do so without self-disgust or wishing I was dead. I no longer feel that death would be preferable to the pain.

The story is not yet finished. When young, I sought serenity and yearned for maturity. I thought that was how you left pain behind. Now I know that even if we could leave our own pain behind, we will still have to live with the pain of others, their hurts, their sorrows, their griefs. If we pretend those don't exist, we are dead somewhere inside ourselves. But equally if we do not recognize that the hurts, the sorrows and the griefs can become the source of courage, of humour and of a blazing, incandescent capacity to love and celebrate life we have missed the point and missed an opportunity.

References

CHAPTERS 1 and 2 PAGES 6–43

W. B. Yeats, *The Second Coming*, in *Selected Poetry*, ed. A. N. Jeffares (London: Macmillan, 1962).

L. Mumford, *The Conduct of Life* (New York: Harcourt Brace, 1951).

D. Morris, *Bodywatching* (London: Cape, 1985).

Virgil, *The Aeneid*, ed. J. W. Mackail, Book 1, Line 462.

S. Fromberg Schaeffer, *The Madness of a Seduced Woman* (London: Pan Books, 1985) p. 174.

E. Matchett, *Journeys of Nothing in the Land of Everything* (Turnstone Books, 1975).

C. MacDougall, *Nocturne one*, in Words/2, Spring 1977.

M. Konner, *The Tangled Wing* (Harmondsworth: Penguin, 1984) p. 302 *et passim*.

J. Liedloff, *The Continuum Concept* (London: Penguin, 1986) p. 73 *et passim*.

J. Kirkland, *Crying and Babies* (Beckenham: Croom Helm, 1985) p. 65 *et passim*.

S. S. Tomkins, *Affect Imagery Consciousness* (London: Tavistock, 1963) Vol. 2.

J. Hoffman, 'Rendezvous' from *Mink Coat* (New York: Holt, Rinehart and Winston, 1969).

CHAPTER 3 PAGES 44–60

H. W. Pullen, *Pueris Reverentia* (Salisbury: Brown and Co., 1892).

N. Gale, *More Cricket Songs* (London: A. Rivers, 1905).

S. Askew and C. Ross, *Boys Don't Cry* (Milton Keynes: Open University Press, 1988).

J. Nicholson, *Men and Women: How Different Are They?* (Oxford: Oxford University Press, 1984).

D. Kuhn, S. C. Nash, L. Bruchan, 'Sex-Role Concepts of two and three year olds', *Child Development*, 49, 1978.

C. E. Ross, J. Mirowski, 'Men Who Cry', *Social Psychology Quarterly*, 1984, 47, 2, pp. 138–46.

J. O. Balswick and C. W. Peek, 'The Inexpressive Male: A Tragedy of American Society', in A. Skolnick and J. H. Skolnick (eds), *Intimacy, Family and Society* (Boston: Little, Brown, 1974).

C. Darwin, *The Expression of the Emotions in Man and Animals* (Chicago: Chicago University Press, 1965).

N. Ephron, *Heartburn* (London: Heinemann, 1983) pp. 87–8.

J. R. Mellow, *Invented Lives: a biography of Scott and Zelda Fitzgerald* (London: Souvenir Press, 1985) pp. 105, 109.

F. Gershon, *Sweetie Baby Cookie Honey* (London: Grafton Books, 1988) p. 550.

CHAPTER 4 PAGES 61–79

I. Murdoch, *Henry and Cato* (London: Chatto and Windus, 1976) p. 60.
Cato, quoted in the *Malleus Maleficarum*, Part 1.
E. B. Browning, 'To George Sand, A Desire', in *Poetical Works of Elizabeth Barrett Browning* (London: Smith, Elder and Co., 1890) vol. III.
Micah, 1.8.

CHAPTER 5 PAGES 80–106

A. de Toqueville, *Democracy in America*, ed. J. P. Mayer (New York: Doubleday, Anchor Books, 1969) p. 508.
A. Haley, *Roots* (London: Hutchinson, 1977).
G. Bedell, *Independent*, 23.3.88.
Colin White, *Independent*, 23.3.88.
J. Haines, *Maxwell* (London: Macdonald, 1988) p. 20.
S. Cook, *Second Life* (London: Michael Joseph, 1982) pp. 177, 230.
B. Bishop, *A Time to Heal* (Sevenoaks: New English Library, 1989) p. 55.
C. Heginbotham, *Social Work Today*, 25.5.87.
H. Yglesias, *Sweetsir* (Sevenoaks: Coronet Books, Hodder and Stoughton, 1982).
O. Wilde, 'The Ballad of Reading Gaol' in *Victorian Prose and Poetry* (Oxford: Oxford University Press, 1973) p. 710.
B. Masters, *Killing For Company, The Case of Denis Nilsen* (Sevenoaks: Coronet Books, Hodder and Stoughton, 1985) p. 185.

CHAPTER 6 PAGES 107–28

J. Sweeney, *Observer*, 15.4.89.
Voltaire, *Lettres sur Oedipe*.
R. Rendell, *The Face of Trespass* (London: Arrow Books, 1975).
D. Spungen, *And I Don't Want to Live This Life* (London: Corgi Books, 1984) p. 320.
T. S. Eliot, 'Little Gidding' from 'Four Quartets', *The Complete Poems and Plays of T. S. Eliot*, (London: Faber and Faber, 1969) pp. 194–5.

CHAPTER 7 PAGES 129–37

F. F. Hvidberg, *Weeping and Laughing in the Old Testament*, trs. L. J. Brill (Leiden, 1962)
H. Kramer and J. Sprenger, *Malleus Maleficarum* (London: Arrow Books, 1971) p. 474.
A. J. Hebert, S.M., *The Tears of Mary and Fatima* (Paulina, La., privately published, 1983) p. 20 *et passim*.
Catherine of Siena, *The Dialogue*, trans. by Suzanne Hoffke, OOP, (New York: Paulist, 1980) p. 170.

CHAPTER 8 PAGES 138-54

H. Ibsen, *Peer Gynt* (London: J. M. Dent and Sons Ltd., 1921) p. 205.

Dante, *The Inferno*, Canto xxx 1.9.

Lord Tennyson, 'The Princess', in *The Poems of Tennyson, 1830–1865* (London: Cassell and Co., 1907) p. 367.

A. Cameron Macdonald, 'Measurement in Angio-neurotic Oedema', *Journal of Psychosomatic Research*, 1964, 8, pp. 207–11.

C. L. Cooper, 'Personality, Life Stress and Cancerous Disease', in *Handbook of Life Stress, Cognition and Health*, ed. S. Fisher and J. Reason (Chichester: John Wiley and Sons, 1988) pp. 369–81.

C. L. Cooper and R. F. Davies Cooper, 'A Prospective Study of the Relationship between Breast Cancer and Life Events, Type A Behaviour, Social Support and Coping Skills' in *Stress Medicine*, 1986, 2, pp. 271–7.

C. L. Cooper, Rachel Cooper, E. B. Faragher, 'Incidence and perception of psychosocial stress: the relationship with breast cancer', in *Psychological Medicine*, 1989, 19, pp. 415–22.

B. Martin, *Observer*, 15.7.90.

University of Oregon, School of Public Health Study, quoted in B. Siegal, *Peace, Love and Healing*, (London: Hutchinson 1990) p. 157.

J. Harrison, *Love Your Disease, It's Keeping You Healthy* (London: Angus and Robertson, 1984) pp. 75, 137.

W. Shakespeare, *A Midsummer Night's Dream*, Act 1.

Aristotle, *Poetics*, ed. D. W. Lucas (Oxford: Clarendon Press, 1968).

H. Jackins, *The Human Side of Human Beings, The Theory of Re-evaluation Counseling* (Seattle: Rational Island Publishers, 1964).

A. Janov, *The Primal Scream* (London: Abacus/Sphere Books, 1973).

E. Coué, *Self Mastery Through Conscious Autosuggestion* (London: Allen and Unwin, 1922).

J. Breuer and S. Freud, *Studies on Hysteria* (London: The Hogarth Press and the Institute of Psychoanalysis, 1956) pp. 162–3.

CHAPTERS 9, 10, 11 AND EPILOGUE PAGES 155-95

J. Lifton, *Death in Life: Survivors of Hiroshima* (London: Weidenfeld and Nicolson, 1968).

S. Johnson, quoted in Boswell's *Life of Samuel Johnson* 7.12.1782.

S. Ringen, *The Possibility of Politics* (Oxford: Oxford University Press, 1987).

C. Wiseman, *The Barbarian File* (Ontario: Sesame Press, 1974) p. 11.

E. Sitwell, *Taken Care Of* (London: Hutchinson, 1965).

V. E. Frankl, *Man's Search for Meaning* (New York: Pocket Books, 1963) pp. 118–19.

S. Kierkegaard, 'Life', quoted in *Bartlett's Familiar Quotations* (London: Macmillan, 1968).

A. Camus, *The Myth of Sisyphus* (Harmondsworth: Penguin Books Ltd., 1975) p. 35.

D. K. Reynolds, *The Quiet Therapies: Japanese Pathways to Personal Growth* (Honolulu: University Press of Hawaii, 1980).

Bibliography and Suggestions for Further Reading

Amnesty International, *Torture in the Eighties* (Oxford: Martin Robertson and Co., 1984).

A. Antonovsky, *Health, Stress and Coping* (London: Josey Boss, 1979).

S. Askew and C. Ross, *Boys Don't Cry* (Milton Keynes: Open University Press, 1988).

J. O. Balswick and C. W. Peek, 'The Inexpressive Male: A Tragedy of American Society' in A. Skolnick and J. H. Skolnick (eds), *Intimacy, Family and Society* (Boston: Little, Brown, 1974).

E. Becker, *The Birth and Death of Meaning* (New York: The Free Press, 1971).

B. Bishop, *A Time to Heal* (Sevenoaks: New English Library, 1989).

D. Bindra, 'Weeping: A Problem of Many Facets' *Bulletin of the British Psychological Society*, 25, 1972, pp. 281–4.

S. Cook, *Second Life* (London: Michael Joseph, 1982).

C. L. Cooper, (ed.), *Stress and Breast Cancer* (Chichester: John Wiley and Sons, 1988).

J. Dunn, *Distress and Comfort* (London: Open Books, 1977).

J. Emsley, 'Chemistry in Tears', *New Scientist*, 16.7.87.

M. Fox, *Original Blessing*, (Santa Fe, New Mexico: Bear and Co., 1983).

V. E. Frankel, *Man's Search for Meaning* (New York: Pocket Books, 1963).

W. H. Frey II, *Crying: The Mystery of Tears* (Minneapolis: Winston Press, 1985).

W. H. Frey II, D. DeSota-Johnson, C. Hoffman, J. T. McCall, 'Effect of Stimulus on the Chemical Composition of Human Tears', in *The American Journal of Opthalmology*, 1981, 92:4, pp. 554–67.

J. Harrison, *Love Your Disease, It's Keeping You Healthy* (London: Angus and Robertson, 1984).

J. Hillman, *Archetypal Psychology* (Dallas, Texas: Spring Publications, 1988).

H. Jackins, *The Human Side of Human Beings, The Theory of Re-evaluation Counseling* (Seattle: Rational Island Publishers, 1964).

A. Janov, *Prisoners of Pain* (London: Abacus, 1982).

S. Jennings (ed.), *Dramatherapy, Theory and Practice for Teachers and Clinicians* (London: Routledge, 1988).

J. Kirkland, *Crying and Babies* (Beckenham: Croom Helm, 1985).

M. Konner, *The Tangled Wing* (Harmondsworth: Penguin, 1984).

P. Krystal, *Cutting The Ties That Bind* (Wellingborough: Turnstone Press, 1982).

J. Lazarre, *On Loving Men* (London: Virago, 1981).

J. Liedloff, *The Continuum Concept* (London: Penguin, 1976) p. 73 *et passim*.

R. J. Lifton, *Death in Life: Survivors of Hiroshima* (London: Weidenfeld and Nicolson, 1968).

J. R. Macy, *Despair and Personal Power in the Nuclear Age* (Philadelphia: New Society Publishers, 1983).

J. A. Mangan, *The Games Ethic and Imperialism* (Harmondsworth: Viking, 1986).

J. A. Mangan, *Athleticism in the Victorian and Edwardian Public Schools* (Cambridge: Cambridge University Press, 1981).

L. de Mause, (ed.), *The History of Childhood* (London: Souvenir Press, 1976).

A. Miller, *For Your Own Good: Hidden Cruelty in Child-Rearing and the Roots of Violence* trans. H. and H. Hannum (London: Faber and Faber, 1983).

C. Murray Parkes, *Bereavement, Studies of Grief in Adult Life* (London: The Tavistock Institute of Human Relations, 1986).

J. Nicholson, *Men and Women: How Different Are They?* (Oxford: Oxford University Press, 1984).

R. Norwood, *Women Who Love Too Much* (London: Arrow Books, 1986).

D. K. Reynolds, *The Quiet Therapies: Quiet Pathways to Personal Growth* (Honolulu: University Press of Hawaii, 1980).

D. K. Reynolds, *Playing Ball on Running Water* (London: Sheldon Press, 1985).

J. Rowan, *The Horned God, Feminism and Men as Wounding and Healing* (London: Routledge and Kegan Paul, 1987).

H. R. Schaffer, *The Growth of Sociability* (London: Penguin, 1971).

T. J. Scheff, *Catharsis in Healing, Ritual and Drama* (London: University of California Press, 1979).

M. Scott Peck, *The Different Drum* (London: Simon and Schuster, 1988).

K. Sherrod, P. Vietze, S. Friedman, *Infancy* (London: Wadsworth, 1978).

B. S. Siegel, *Love, Medicine and Miracles* (London: Rider/Century Hutchinson, 1986).

E. and G. Strachan, *Freeing the Feminine* (Dunbar: Labarum Publications, 1985).

A. Tolson, *The Limits of Masculinity* (London: Tavistock Publications, 1977).

S. S. Tomkins, *Affect Imagery Consciousness* (London: Tavistock Publications, 1963) Vol. 2.

J. Turner, *A Crying Game, The Diary of a Battered Wife* (Edinburgh: Mainstream Publishing, 1984).

D. G. Williams, 'Weeping by Adults: Personality Correlates and Sex Differences', *The Journal of Psychology*, 110, 1982, pp. 217–26.

K. Wybar and M. K. Muir, *Opthalmology* (New York: Balliere Tindall, 1984).

I. D. Yalom, *Existential Psychotherapy* (New York: Basic Books, 1980).

Index of People and Places

I have not attempted to compile an index of concepts related to feelings such as anger, fear, shame, tenderness or joy. These are so deeply woven into the text as to make the task impossible and the result absurd. Major themes, like grief and health, together with the people and ideas associated with them, are accessible through chapter headings. Of equal significance, although not identified in a chapter heading, are issues concerned with children. These will be found in Chapter Two but for those who choose to hear, resonate throughout the text.